FALMOUTH

574 · 9719

 CORNWALL COUNTY LIBRARY

COUNTY HALL

TRURO   Tel. 4282

Beyond
the North Wind

Also by the Author:

BOOKS

Nature Realms Across America
Crosses in the Wind
Birdlife of Virginia
Guidelines to Conservation Education Action
Open Land for Urban America
Birdlife of Del-Mar-Va
Nature Centers in America

BOOKLETS

Game Birds, Mammals, Fish of Virginia
Fishlife of Virginia
A Look at Virginia's Natural Resources
Wild Animal Tracks

MANUALS (for the National Audubon Society)
A Nature Center for Your Community
A Manual of Outdoor Conservation Education
Wildlife Habitat Improvement (co-authored with Byron
L. Ashbaugh and Con D. Tolman)
Manual of Outdoor Interpretation

Beyond
the North Wind

Joseph James Shomon

South Brunswick and New York: A. S. Barnes and Company
London: Thomas Yoseloff Ltd

© 1974 by A. S. Barnes and Co., Inc.

A. S. Barnes and Co., Inc.
Cranbury, New Jersey 08512

Thomas Yoseloff Ltd
108 New Bond Street
London W1Y OQX, England

Library of Congress Cataloging in Publication Data

Shomon, Joseph James, 1914-
  Beyond the north wind.

  1. Natural history—Arctic regions. 2. Arctic regions—Description
and travel. I. Title.
QH84.1.S47   574.9719   73-124
ISBN 0-498-01283-2.

Printed in the United States of America

To Vera (Vee Bee)
Wife, helpmate, and traveling companion

Contents

Foreword

The Arctic is one of the last great remaining worlds of nature still relatively unspoiled. Because this region is circumpolar in geography, many nations have continental ownership here and many others also strong interests. The Canadian Northwest Territories occupy an enormous part of the Arctic, as does Alaska, Greenland, and the Soviet Union, and so various governments are interested and concerned about what happens here. From a wildlife standpoint the North American Arctic, especially the tundra region, is key to the survival and management of so much of our waterfowl and other migrating birds as well as the Barren Ground caribou, musk-ox, and polar bear. We must protect and manage these and other natural resources wisely, for not even the Arctic today is free from man's propensity toward overexploitation.

One of the big needs at present is for more scientific data and more accurate general information on the Arctic world, its character, nature of life, and carrying capacities, both for animals and humans. We already know that the Arctic tundra is an enormously fragile ecosystem and man's activities there must be tempered with caution and wisdom.

Now comes another book on the world of the Far North, but a different kind of a book. Dr. Shomon is not only an observant wildlife biologist and environmental planner but also an extensive traveler and sensitive writer who has tried to picture the Arctic world as he has seen it. Written in a free and easy journalistic style rather than the hand of a pedant, his feeling and descriptions come through vividly.

Appearing at a time of worldwide environmental concern, *Beyond the North Wind* should do much for the layman as well as the serious minded in portraying a clearer ecological picture of a great and fascinating region.

Dr. Ira N. Gabrielson
Former President, Wildlife Management Institute and Honorary President, The World Wildlife Fund

Preface

Occasional glimpses of a passing wilderness from a train window. The exposed Canadian Shield on a windswept point where the waters of a big river intermingle with cold Hudson Bay. A place where white whales wallow. A golden plover feigning a broken-wing act. A phalarope twirling in a lakelet festooned with blooming cottongrass. The howls of timber wolves in the coniferous taiga. Moose and marten, Indians and Eskimos. Naked rocks and shaggy musk-ox and glistening ice and snow. Polar bear and seal and the strange and remarkable life of the roving Barren Ground caribou. These and other haunting scenes come to the mind's eye to reconstruct the face of the Arctic tundra—a vast natural domain, free and wild and challenging—where all living things and all that's classed as nonliving show the telltale marks of a hostile land.

In this kind of a trying world I have chosen to do my sojourning, first as a scientist bent on separating truth from fiction, second as an adventurer seeking the feeling and fascination of another land, and third as a photographer and writer attempting to record what the Arctic is really like. There is yet a fourth reason for these sojourns, an answer I often give to my mother when she asks: "But why do you go to such a dreadful place?" and to which I invariably respond: "And why do men go to the wilds of the Amazon? Why do they attempt to climb Everest?"

One goes to the Far North, I suppose, because it is there, because it is still largely unblemished, wild, and full of mystery, full

11

of challenges. As a forester-biologist I find unpeopled places tempting and joyous, for I recall that it was Albert Einstein who once said, "When the mysterious goes out of a man's life, that man is dead." I count myself among the fortunate who still find zest, deep meaning, and pleasure in unspoiled nature; and the wondrous and mysterious can still be found on our planet for those who seek it.

My purpose in writing this book is simple: to bring some fresh insight to the reader on the northland, to correct many of the misimpressions that people have about the Arctic, and to help foster a better appreciation of the natural tundra world and its life. The Arctic, and especially the tundra world, is no longer completely safe from the relentless encroachments of civilization, no more than are the other major ecosystems of the North American continent. The wildness of the Far North is passing and, should it go, the great cosmic wisdom we find there can pass from the face of our land—and man and all life that share this living planet with that world will be that much poorer for it.

—Joseph James Shomon

Beyond
the North Wind

1
Beyond the North Wind

High up on the forehead of our twirling globe, between the stunted taiga forests and the Arctic Sea, sprawls a formidable land that belongs to nature. It is a remorseless land where everything spells struggle and much that's visible bears the telltale marks of a hostile world. This is the Arctic tundra—the land beyond the North Wind.

The tundra is an enormously big place, filled with countless shimmering lakes and great ice-packed rivers, a place of much bleakness and sameness. Yet it is a world that at times seethes with abundant life.

The tundra is the world of the lemming and lichen, the loon and the longspur, the wandering ice bear and the Arctic Barren Ground grizzly. It is, above all else, a land that belongs to wild nature —the raw elements like the wind and the cold and incredible creatures like the musk-ox and the roving Barren Ground caribou.

In North America the tundra begins where the open boreal wilderness, the taiga, ends. To the discerning eye it unfolds piecemeal, at first allowing one only a glimpse of it. Eventually it opens up wide, stretching out, expanseful in a never-ending frozen plain. This is the country of frigid winters and much darkness, of long, sunlit summer days and brief weeks of flourishing life, the home of the ptarmigan and the white wolf, of small, brown-skinned men and the great ice bear they call Goliath of the frozen North.

To the frequent sojourner to these lands the tundra is a montage of many images—of mirrored lakes and sparkling lakelets, of rustling ice and innumerable eskers, of gravelly hills and hillocks and sandy mounds, where the sik-sik loves to play. It is lonesome lowlands, some dry, some moist, where shaggy creatures graze in silence and where a gallant goose, the snow goose, comes to make its home.

The tundra world is color and change. It is glistening coastal ice and shiny snowbanks and shadowy glacial ridges; it is the outpouring of lakes with green rivers sparkling out like champagne from overfilled crystal chalices, and it is the oozing out of snow water from hills of granite and limestone. It is the yellow lichen on the glacial erratic, one and a dozen and a hundred times a dozen, all strewn about and heaved out by the permafrost.

The tundra realm is a compelling place. Like some mysterious magnet it draws life to it, restless birds from another clime with their endless preparation and ceaseless performance compatible with nesting and the raising of new families. It is long-tailed jaegers and pace-setting terns and owls, silent and swooping, and carrying a plumage white as Arctic snow.

To the followers of wildlife the tundra is a big northern stage, ever revolving and changing, a moving turntable with many star performers. The shows are the scampering of mice over the crowberries, the wanderings of lemmings from crowded tunnels beneath the snow, the sniffing of an Arctic grizzly as he checks the air for fresh whiffs of roving caribou. It is the evening *ket ket* of the rock ptarmigan as he struts around the cottongrass and the song of the orange-eyed wolf as he surveys from a windswept esker a vast domain of seeming nothingness. It is ageless pathways over the grasslands, deep furrows numbering a hundred and ten times a hundred, straight and curving, all flowing endlessly north across the landscape. It is the eerie laughter of a sharp-billed bird on a lake in the long evening glow and the distant rumble of wild ugulates as thousands of hooves respond to an ageless calling in the Arctic night.

The tundra world is part of a still larger world—the vast domain that is the Arctic. This region proper includes not only that huge expanse of tundra land from 66 degrees 30 minutes north latitude to the Arctic Ocean but also the islands and the frigid waters and pack ice north to the North Pole. While the Arctic Circle demarcation is purely mathematical and primarily useful in navigational and astronomical studies, the true Arctic embraces all the lands and waters above the treeline—an uneven line north and south of the Arctic Circle above which no trees live—to the earth's true north pole. Enormously big, it is a region that covers more than eight million square miles, an area nearly three times the size of continental United States.

The Arctic region is circumpolar, sweeping across Alaska, Canada, Greenland, Norway, Sweden, Finland, and Russia. Most people think of the area around the North Pole as land caked by snow and ice. But this part of the Arctic is not land but water that is perpetually frozen over to make up the polar ice pack. Beneath this ever-changing ice mass—really an island of ice—is the central Arctic Sea marked by a deep basin with a high subterranean ridge running through it. The coastal land dips into this sea through the continental shelves, which are said to be the longest in the world. These underwater projections are especially long in Russia where they extend outward in places as much as eight hundred miles. The central basin of the Arctic Sea has recently been chartered and measures roughly seven hundred to fourteen hundred miles and is up to six thousand feet deep; some sea chasms, however, extend downward as much as fifteen thousand feet. In contrast, the Hudson Bay is a shallow body of water and averages only six hundred fifty feet in depth.

One soon finds when traveling in the Arctic that the climate is not all savage and cold. While low temperatures occur in the Arctic, colder temperatures have been recorded in such places as sub-Arctic Siberia, Montana, Minnesota, and even in a frost pocket in northern New York. On the entire Arctic coast—but not the Arctic Archipelago islands at higher latitudes—there is no record of temperatures below −55° F. With the exception of Greenland, which is a land plateau with bordering mountains and much land ice, about nine-tenths of all Arctic lands are free of ice and snow in the summer.

Although winter temperatures in the Arctic have been recorded as low as −90° F, and this in sub-Arctic Siberia, summer temperatures may rise as high as 70° F, even higher. One July day at Fort Yukon, which lies just above the Arctic Circle in Alaska, the temperature rose into the nineties. Summer temperatures in some parts of Alaska, for instance, would be called hot in Tennessee or South Carolina. This is due to the warming waters of the West Wind Drift, which brings warm, central Pacific waters to the western coast of Alaska. Another warming current in the east, the

Fort Yukon, Alaska.

North Atlantic Drift, brings mild weather to western Newfoundland, Iceland, and the northerncoasts of Scandinavia. It is hard to
believe but summer rains, instead of snows, have occurred even at
the North Pole. The average winter temperature for the whole Arctic region is said to be an unbelievable 30° F. Along much of the
Arctic coast, the winds in the summertime usually blow from the
sea and thus feel warmer, while in the winter they blow from the
land and seem much colder.

One also discovers with delight, and especially if he is a forest-
er, that there are extensive forests in the southern Arctic. The
whole circumpolar region along its southern land fringe is marked
by the open boreal forests, the taiga, where primeval stands of
spruce and fir, birch, alder, and willow are found. In Alaska and
the northwestern Canadian sub-Arctic the dominant tree is the
beautifully shaped white spruce. In Labrador and Quebec the main

coniferous tree is the black spruce, but the needle-shedding tamarack or larch also occurs.

Where trees bow to the onslaught of the north winds, soggy ground occurs and dwarf and woody plants take over. In the Arctic prairies where stunted evergreens and Arctic grasses, lichens, and mosses predominate, the chief cause is dryness rather than the cold. Some seventeen hundred different kinds of plants have been identified in the Arctic, including nine hundred distinct wildflowers. These plants furnish food for the caribou, musk-ox, Arctic hare, brown and collared lemming, and other rodents. These mammals in turn furnish food for the Barren Ground grizzly, Arctic wolf, white fox, wolverine, ermine, and some flesh-eating birds.

Drawn to the Arctic seas are a limited number of marine mam-

Pribilof Island fur seals. *Courtesy V. B. Scheffer, U.S. Fish and Wildlife Service.*

mals, such as walrus, seals, and whales, including the white
baluga, the killer whale, and the giant blue whale. The waters must
be partially free of ice for these animals, which means that they are
mostly summer migrants. A few species, like the seal, can remain
around all winter with the help of blow holes. It is the seal that

The author and two Alaskan king salmon.

forms the chief food source for the polar bear. Some 120 kinds of fish are caught in Arctic seas, mostly in sub-Arctic open waters, with halibut, cod, and flounder the principal species. Some salmon, grayling, and Arctic char are also taken.

Perhaps the most intriguing aspect of the Arctic is its bird life. Places like Churchill, on Hudson Bay, the sea islands of the eastern Canadian Archipelago, and the Yukon Delta, are favorite gathering areas for nesting birds and thereby constitute an ornithologist's paradise.

Some of the birds in the Far North are used for food by the Eskimos and Indians. The most abundant birds in Arctic lands are waterfowl, ravens, falcons, snowbirds, and sandpipers. Ptarmigan are common on the open tundra. Puffins, petrels, and auks nest on the sea islands and lowlands along the coast. Murres, dovekies, gulls, and sea pigeons nest along the Arctic cliffs.

One small marsh bird, the sora, finds the Arctic tundra its principal nesting home. This awkward rail, appearing very much like a tiny flightless chicken—and in the air looking like a bunch of rags—flies south from the Hudson Bay region in the fall all the way to the freshwater marshes of eastern United States.

Several common summer Arctic residents fly southward incredible distances. These birds are not content to stop in northern South America but push on across the Equator and on down to the pampas of Argentina.

Of all North American land birds, one group has the longest migration route of all. The birds of this group fly to the Yukon Territory and Alaska in the summer, then migrate south in the winter to Argentina—seven thousand miles away. The seasonal flights of some birds are exceeded in length by the journeys of several species of water birds, principally members of the suborder of shore birds. In this group are found nineteen species that nest north of the Arctic Circle and winter in South America. Of this group six species migrate as far south as Patagonia. Thus a number of birds have migration routes of eight thousand miles or more in length.

The champion "globe-trotter" of them all is the Arctic tern. The name *Arctic* is well earned, as the breeding range of this bird is circumpolar, nesting as far north as it can find a suitable place to rear its young. The first nest to be found in the high Arctic was only 7½ degrees from the North Pole. It contained a downy chick encased by a wall of newly fallen snow that had been scooped out by the parent. The Arctic tern in North America seems to breed southward in the interior to Great Slave Lake and on the Atlantic coast to Massachusetts. After the young are grown these birds vanish from their North American breeding grounds only to reappear a few months later in the Antarctic—some eleven thousand miles away. Until very recently the route followed by these strong fliers was a complete mystery. While a few scattered individuals have been noted as far south as Long Island, the species was otherwise practically unknown along the Atlantic coasts of North and South America. It was, however, known to be a migrant along the west coast of Europe and Africa. By means of numbered bands and many records, the picture is now developing that gives the Arctic tern credit for making the most remarkable and longest of all migratory bird journeys in the world.

What is it about the Arctic that attracts birds? What makes the walrus, the beluga, and the killer whale seek out the northern waters? What causes the caribou to move out onto the tundra and roam north over it a hundred, a thousand miles? These are mysteries that defy explanation, although theories and educated guesses there will always be. Perhaps when man is able to explain his own calling to the wild he may be on the threshold of a plausible answer. But why worry? Why be occupied with such trivia? Is it not enough that the Arctic is there, that the tundra unfolds to the setting sun?

I for one am tranquil that nature does not reveal all her secrets, for in that condition the biologist, and particularly the naturalist, finds much of the savor and spirit that lead him onward to discover and learn and in the process come to know the beauty of the natural world and its life.

One thing seems certain—there is a subtle, unexplainable wisdom in wild things that supercedes all human intelligence, an art and design from which man can learn much. From wild nature, from its many actions, co-actions, its perfection, and manifold adaptations, one begins to perceive the deep framework of survival. Indeed in primeval nature lies the secret of survival of our planet and all its ecosystems. One may wonder for a while if this is so, but observing closely an ant hill, the migration of salmon, the territorial ways of birds and mammals, including the remarkable makeup of Arctic animals, it is easily seen that in nature alone lies the hidden mystery and ingredients of life and nonlife. Man through science can discover the power of the atom and technology can apply its use, but only infinite nature can construct and control a living cell. The structure of the hydrogen atom nucleus is simple when compared to the complex composition and workings of the plant or animal cell.

One does not need to travel to the Arctic, of course, to see all this, but it helps. Here primeval nature is more clearly on display, and its lessons are discernible and full of meaning.

2

On Untrodden Trails
in the Sub-Arctic North

The late Professor Dow W. Baxter taught a number of courses in forest pathology at the School of Natural Resources of the University of Michigan. I was one of his students. Everyone, students and faculty, called him Dow and loved him. What was remarkable about Dow was his buoyancy in the outdoors and great zeal for pursuing fungi in the field.

One of Dow's deep loves was Alaska. He worshipped that territory with a passion, like a man loves the town of his birth, and each summer for many years he went on fungi-hunting expeditions to that faraway northland. He was going to write a book someday and he would call it *The Unknown Alaska,* and it would be a book largely in pictures. I don't know if Dow ever got his book published, but I do remember well how he used to extoll that country, especially the high mountains where he sojourned so often. "If you want to know Alaska," I remember him saying many times, "then follow the untrodden trails—and see the Alaskan high ranges."

Thus began my interest in the Far North—in that land beyond the north wind.

Some years later when Alaska was still a territory and the battle for statehood was fresh in everyone's mind, I sojourned up into that big country and decided to see the remote parts of Alaska, as Dow advised. I had come mostly to see big game and study

Alaska's conservation problems. I had no idea I would run into a most cooperative United States Fish and Wildlife Service at various points, especially at Anchorage and Fairbanks. Perhaps being a professional wildlife biologist on a doctoral mission helped some, but I maintain too that the factor of luck in finding people like Jim King had much to do with it.

Jim was a pilot and a nonprofessional biologist assigned to the service at Fairbanks, and his specialty was big-game aerial surveys. When I called upon the local field office of the Fish and Wildlife Service and asked if perchance I might go on an aerial big-game survey, a supervising biologist in charge said almost jokingly, "Sure, do you want to go now?"

But he wasn't joking. If I was ready, Jim King was the man to take me.

Jim was going on a moose census and, well, if things worked out, "there might also be a spin over the high country after white sheep."

It all sounded unbelievable. But soon we were on the runway and Jim radioed back, "Take off!" We dashed away and were promptly over the Chena River and its great green sprawling muskegs.

"We're going southwest toward the Tanana," Jim yelled, "that's moose country. We'll fly transects. Will you tally the moose?"

I nodded and took hold of the tally sheet. It contained lots of square blocks where through a dot system one can record sightings of bulls, cows, and yearlings. Each dot represented one sighting. Our craft was a single-engined Cessna and Jim whipped it around like a toy. "What do you do," I hollered, "when your motor fails? That country down there looks awful wet and messy to me."

Jim smiled and shot back, "This motor doesn't fail—never has yet. Oh, I guess if you had to land, you could pancake okay in those muskegs. But we're not going to have any of that. Look. There's our first moose!"

It took me a while to find it, a small black figure standing in a shallow lakelet and Jim yelled, "Mark one bull."

In another minute we spotted a family of moose, a large antlered bull, a cow, and a calf. Soon more appeared and still more. I was kept busy putting down dots and taking pictures. Soon it seemed as if every large muskeg and every lake held one or more moose. The country was absolutely alive with them.

Now and then Jim decided to get a better look and went down,

The musk-ox on Nunnivak Island in Alaska. *Courtesy Cecil Rhode, U.S. Fish and Wildlife Service.*

swooping across a bunch of startled moose at five hundred feet. Once we surprised a large bull as he was feeding, head completely submerged in the water. As we sallied down, he suddenly heard us and lifted his head out of the water, lily pads, moss, and water streaming down all over him. He was a sight. He shook his large antlers at us and the weeds just flew.

About forty moose later, Jim repeated the surprising maneuver on a large moose group. This time one old father moose didn't like the intrusion one bit. After his head cleared the water he literally jumped up into the air and shook his mighty antlered head at us, water and grass again flying in all directions. We laughed but it was nothing funny to the giant of the muskegs. Had we been on foot, I'm sure we would have been in for some trouble.

For a long time we flew transect lines, always one mile apart, back and forth, counting new moose all the time. Finally, after one hour of tallying, I counted fifty-five moose on our sheet and Jim swung away from the muskegs.

"Let's see if we can find some Dall sheep and caribou," he said. "Have to hit the Alaska Range, that okay?"

I nodded, but was elated beyond description, for I remembered what Dow had said. Now it was time to begin exchanging the game tally sheet for my cameras. In a few minutes we were over some foothills and heavy timber. But the muskegs continued to appear in between the ridge openings. At one point, Jim spotted something and began to circle, pointing.

We were about fifteen hundred feet and started to descend. Then I saw what Jim's sharp eyes had spotted, a lone Alaskan brown bear beside a pool of water. He was jumping in and out of the pool in a playful fashion. We came down over him to about five hundred feet and circled, but he paid no attention to us. He looked like a teddy bear having fun in a basin of water. He just kept jumping in and out. Every time he came out of the water, he rose on his hind feet and shook himself violently, the water flying away from him in all directions. Never once did he seem to mind the noisy

The Alaskan brown bear ranges into the Arctic country. *Courtesy Dick Chace, U.S. Fish and Wildlife Service.*

intrusion from above. Wild animals soon get used to noises, such as an airplane, and apparently pay no attention to them. It is the unusual, the suspicious noise that startles them. Then one must watch out. Such disturbances one should avoid when on foot, for large animals like the brownie or grizzly or even the moose, may sometimes attack. In the plane one feels comfortable and safe enough although in one sense it is not exactly the fairest way to see big game.

We finally left the brownie to his private bathing and headed for the high country, the ridges and high plateaus, and the snowbanks.

As we started climbing the Alaskan Range we began seeing larger and larger patches of snow. The mountains loomed higher and closer and I started to get a funny sensation in my stomach.

"Look for Dall sheep," Jim said. "They should be showing up. They're pure white."

I began scanning the rugged slopes and crags. In about fifteen minutes Jim spotted a small band of cottonlike objects on a precipitous mountainside and headed right toward them, the mountain coming toward us incredibly fast. Then as we got uncomfortably close and the white sheep began scattering up the cliffs he turned the little craft. I sighed.

Soon we were winging low over a high plateau. "There," said Jim pointing. "Look!"

Below us a large band of caribou were running. They were in a stampede and the rocks flew about them. The group numbered about a hundred in all. I tried getting pictures but the whole episode was over in a matter of seconds. Such sights just don't tarry for long.

Soon an enormous mountain loomed ahead and Jim turned our plane into a massive deep canyon. Now snow was on all sides and the air became very bumpy. At times the ups and downs were so violent we fell or jumped a hundred feet. As the canyon curved, so did we, Jim cruising through the narrow passageway like through some ice gorge. I kept taking pictures, movies and stills, and when I was least expecting it, the plane would either suddenly drop or Jim would turn quickly from a looming ice wall. I felt my stomach give. It was too much. On the next drop my stomach did a somersault and up came my dinner. Thank goodness I caught it in my handkerchief.

"Oh, I'm sorry," Jim said.

"No, no, it's all right," I said. "It's only those turns, and downdrafts."

Mendenhall Glacier, Juneau, Alaska.

It was good that I was game, for then came one of the great experiences of my life. Jim turned the nose of our Cessna toward the snowfields and glaciers and we began a slow climb toward a fantastic icy white no-man's land—a country of bristling ivory peaks, jagged precipices, and avenues of mighty ice and snow. The view was stupendous and fiercely wild.

I happened to glance at the gas gauge. It was below half full. Jim noticed it too. All kinds of terrible thoughts flashed through my mind, but I tried only thinking of the spectacular beauty all around us. For several long minutes we cruised through this high world of fantasy, up one ice canyon, over another bristling peak, across another snowfield. Would Jim find his way out? Great Heavens, this was no place for such a small plane. The frightful thoughts came on fast but I just clamped my jaws and held my breath. The feeling was one of terror and joy. We were on top of the world in sub-Arctic Alaska and the scenes were all stark nature—ice, glaciers, sharp peaks, jagged snowy crags.

I felt my face turning green again and for a minute the horrible feeling in my stomach once again took away all that was beautiful.

Jim saw my condition and began to turn the craft around, to my great relief. Now I prayed that God would show us the way out. Jim looked confident. It was a slow, thrilling return journey. My prayers were answered, and soon we were out of the worst of it and headed for the low country.

Forty minutes later I climbed out of the plane at Fairbanks. One of the game biologists there asked me how I liked the trip. I only shook my head trying to catch my breath. "Greatest thrill of my life," I finally said, "the very greatest!"

For a very long time, this trip over the muskegs and high ranges in Alaska indelibly impressed my memory. Little wonder the Northland keeps calling you back—again and again.

Since that deeply moving trip over those high sub-Arctic mountains I have thought about it many times. Jim King went on to finish his college after that and received a degree in wildlife man-

The author in sub-Arctic Alaska.

Drying fish along the Kosquoquim River in Alaska.

agement. Then he went back to the Fish and Wildlife Service as a biologist with tours of duty at Nome and Juneau, Alaska.

I've seen Jim King several times since that day in Fairbanks and we always talk about that trip.

"There are only two ways to see the North country and it's wild-life," Jim would say. "You see it from a small plane at closer range or better yet, you sojourn over the country on foot. Aerial forays are good but nothing will beat seeing the land and its wild-life like pushing into the bush on your own two feet. . .," and he hesitated, ". . .and hitting the untrodden trail."

Not long after my Alaska sojourn with Jim King, I was doing just what Jim advocated—hitting the bush in the Yukon Territory bent on seeing more wildlife. The Yukon country is sandwiched between the vastness of Alaska on the left and the great expanse of the Northwest Territories on the right. It is the country of the

Klondike—the fabulous region of the Gold Rush that made history about the turn of the century. Indeed, the difficult and trying years of the fortune seekers—those arduous trips up from Skagway and on across White Pass to Lake Bennett and then down the Yukon River to Whitehorse—were moments of great colorful history. The new gold strikes on the Klondike and its tributaries, the plying steamers between Whitehorse and the Klondike, all were days of great excitement, great valor, and great tragedy. Here in this north-land, the setting of Robert Service's immortal "The Cremation of Sam McGee," the spirit of the wilderness lives on.

The Yukon Territory is one vast rugged wilderness, a wilderness in its truest sense with trees everywhere, and with rivers and mountains and lakes that are gorgeous. Unlike the tundra of the central Canadian barrens, the Yukon country is able to support tree growth because of the warming influences of the McKenzie River to the east and its accompanying McKenzie Mountains and the Chinook winds that blow up from the southwest across Alaska and British Columbia. Too cold for agriculture, yet possessing a sufficient growing season for conifers, the Yukon Territory presents suitable conditions for a forested wilderness. Nowhere else in North America is a large, single political subdivision of land so extensively and beautifully forested. In ecological terms this great north-land country is a superb sub-Arctic forested wilderness—the acme of the sprawling, sweeping, great Canadian Hudsonian Forest.

Every country and every land has its special characteristics, its representative plants and animals. The Yukon has its own. The dominant trees are confiers, mostly white spruce. The representative animals are white sheep (Dall sheep), moose, beaver, bear, fisher, marten, and a rarely seen creature, the wolverine, which is about as tough as any animal alive.

The taxonomists call this big member of the weasel family *Gulo luscus,* the French Canadian trappers speak of him as *Carcajou* or the stealing skunk bear. Some northern Indians and Eskimos think of him as the *fiercest one.* While I will not go so far as to call the wolverine bad names, I will say he is fearless, and clever almost to the point of being cunning. What's more, he is remarkably ingenious in habit. Any animal that can upset a batch of freshly set traps and drive a trapper mad is deserving of some special adjectives. However, I must say in all candor that the few I have seen in the wild all seemed to be in bad temper. Nevertheless, there is much in this creature that is to be admired. For one thing, he's strong, he's bold, and he's absolutely fearless!

The author at Barrow, Alaska.

Gulo is unique in one special sense—he will not retreat or give ground to any wild animal on this continent or even in the Old World where he is also found. I'm speaking, of course, in situations of a fair match and not of a hunter with a gun and a pack of dogs.

One summer I saw a wolverine in a burrow along the ice at Barrow, Alaska, and all I saw when I came close was a black face and lots of flashing, chattering teeth. The hissing and growling was merely the uninviting frosting on the cake. Needless to say I gave this fellow plenty of quick tundra space between us.

Just as the wolf personifies wilderness, so too the wolverine represents stark wildness. In my journal book Gulo is the wildest of wild animal fighters of the North American continent, ranking in courage and ferocity to the tiger of India and the leopard of Africa. Moreover, if what the researchers say at the Arctic Research Institute at Barrow, Alaska, is true, and of this I have no doubt, then the wolverine is one mammal that can never be tamed in captivity.

Gulo's range is the upper half of the great Hudsonian Forest, the sparsely forested taiga, and the Arctic barrens, including Baffin Island, and some of the islands of the Arctic Archipelago. A few of his kind range the mountains of the Rockies south to Colorado, but here they are very scarce.

What does Gulo look like? Picture a squattish, bearlike animal, brown to black in color and with heavy limbs, all in a body measuring from two to three feet, plus a fifteen-inch tail that is very bushy. Visualize further a twenty-to forty-pound bundle of long fur moving so fast as to be able to catch a marmot unawares, and you have lumped into one four-foot package a much-to-be-respected wolverine. When a stranger meets such a mass of strength and ferocity on a trail on a dark afternoon, be he man or another beast, the adrenalin is bound to soar.

I recall an encounter in the Yukon that sent my own adrenalin

Eskimos blanket tossing at Point Barrow, Alaska.

soaring to dizzy heights, an event so poignant that unless one was actually an eyewitness, he would find it difficult to believe. I was hitting the trail of the Yukon River above Whitehorse one day intent on trying for some grayling in the river's rapids. The fishing didn't pay off and since there was still good light, I decided to hike up to the gorge and get some scenic pictures. I finally made it to where a swinging foot bridge dangles dangerously over the narrow river's gorge and took my pictures. I then decided to explore more of the trail country northward. After going perhaps a mile further up the river, I was suddenly stopped by a terrific commotion on the river bank below me. I could not see the spot where all the screaming and growling was taking place, so I dropped low and crawled to the trail's bank and took concealment behind a clump of low spruces.

The noise continued: much hissing and the sound of flying gravel. There was so much tearing about and growling that I knew that two animals had met in a surprising encounter. Such a meeting cannot be considered too surprising in this country since the trail at both levels of the river bank is very narrow. Obviously it was made by caribou and bear, but when two animals met, they would have to either give ground or fight for the right of way.

I edged to another clump of spruces and raised my head slowly and was astonished by the scene. There, not fifty feet away, two furred animals were sparring, circling, and making menacing gestures toward one another. One was a wolf, a large, gray, almost ash-colored specimen, the other appeared to be a dark wolverine, hugging the ground with his belly and making fearsome rushes toward his opponent. At first glance this second fellow looked like a badger, but when he spun around in lightninglike fashion and I saw his full size, there was no mistaking him. He was a full-blooded wolverine and all fight.

I was so overcome by this incredible sight—the most fiercely dramatic sight in animaldom I had ever seen in the wild—that I could scarcely breathe, let alone reach for my camera. Could I be imagining all this? Was it really happening? It was for real all right, and the two battlers were making no bones about it. Then and there, in a flash of observation, I gained a deeper and more profound respect for these animals. Here they were, both courageous beasts of the wilderness, each strong and powerful, testing their wild ways one against the other. Had the wolf an ounce of softness in him he would have broken off the engagement. But no, he was not giving in an inch. Meanwhile, his much smaller, ground-hugging adversary, half as small and hardly a third as tall, was not yielding a hair and was showing it.

For a full minute I glued my eyes on the scene. No body contact had been made but yet I could tell that one was imminent. No sooner had I thought of this than the wolverine flew at his opponent, throwing his full body against the wolf's neck and shoulder, tearing away great chunks of fur. But the wolf tore back at his attacker and shook him off with one savage shake of his head. The two broke off contact instantly and again resumed their sparring positions on the trail. The wolf was bleeding from the muzzle and lips and when his head turned around toward the sunlight his eyes for a split second shone like two orange flames. I've seen wild wolves but this was the wildest one I've ever seen, so fierce he was really beautiful.

Once more the wolverine spit at him and slammed the earth with his front feet, first one, then the other, then both, and growling with every rush forward, feigning an attack. The wolf saw his chance at one point and lunged forward but was short by inches, the wolverine springing just out of reach and then himself sailing once more into the wolf. This time the wolf and wolverine were all mixed up in one loud, growling bedlam, blood and fur and saliva flying around, bodies tumbling and rolling and tearing up the gravel, rocks flying. I tried to reach for my camera and stepped on a loose rock, and it went tumbling down to the bank, bouncing as it went. The combatants sensed that something was wrong and broke off their contact. In an instant they separated and sped on their separate ways in opposite directions on the trail. Once again a rare encounter in the wild was suddenly interrupted by a man, and nature was not allowed to finish her example of stark violence. I was left completely stunned. But I soon recovered and then began to feel lucky in having seen this much of the epic struggle.

All during the time of that encounter, it seemed, I had stopped breathing. Now that it was over and I could breathe normally again I spotted a nice restful looking boulder and ambled over to it, then took in deep breaths. So absorbed was my mind with the battle, so utterly immersed had I become in a different world, that for a time at least I was completely oblivious to everything. I had dropped my hat somewhere and had not missed it until now. I was also bleeding from a big scratch that some bush had made and was oblivious to this too.

While I had muffed a once-in-a-lifetime camera shot and there would be no record on film, there was a record indelibly impressed in my memory—one that will live on for the rest of my days.

I once had a genial boss who loved to hunt wild turkeys and quail. I. T. Quinn was his name. He was, for a long time, the executive director of the Virginia Fish and Game Commission. Most people called him I. T. and often I recall hearing him say, usually in some speech before a game club, how he was going to write a book someday.

"What will be the title of your book," I asked him at one such occasion.

"Well, I'll tell you," he said, "I will call that book *The Shots which I have missed.* I'm *proud* of *those* shots; they'll linger in my memory always."

I too will carry in my memory the mental picture of a wolf and wolverine sparring on a trail in the sub-Arctic Yukon wilderness and wondering, as one must always wonder, how it happened in the first place, what would have occurred if I didn't pull that boo-boo, and whether these two marvelous creatures of the wild ever had reason to meet again.

The great northern bush is replete with surprises and full of meaning. I know for one that it has taught me many things —foremost, perhaps, is the deep sense of wonder and beauty in the wild, and in that sense, I believe, lies much of the joy that gladdens the heart of the wandering naturalist.

3
The Taiga and the Tundra

The chilly North Wind whispered softly, almost melodiously, through the clump of stunted spruces, and the sun, a red-eyed Cyclops, hung low over the bay, casting a golden glow over the sprawling taiga. I was sitting on top of a low glacial esker and had my field glasses trained on a lakelet where tiny ripples were coming from a twirling bird. Above and beyond the water's edge the soggy ground was ablaze with spring wildflowers, shades of gold and lavender, and punctuated here and there were clumps of blooming white cottongrass.

The bird was a northern phalarope, a kind of a sandpiper, and his beak dipped into the water in quick fashion as he turned round and round. As I lowered my binoculars to gain a better look he stopped spinning, grew suspicious, and burst from the water. I followed him with my glasses as he winged low over the treeless tundra past small islands of wind-beaten evergreens, only to disappear in another wet area. It was a pleasant scene—the swish of the wind across the dwarfed spruces, the phalarope twirling, the open barrens splashed with soft colors in the sun's evening glow, all conjuring a moment in time that became deeply etched in my memory. This was the country of the blending of two fragile environments, the taiga and the tundra, the subarctic land just south of the land beyond the North Wind.

This was the country in the sub-Arctic that Arthur Fuller told me

Nesting site of the northern phalarope near Churchill.

about. "You must go there," I remembered him saying, "it's worth seeing." Then beaming as he recollected his own experiences at Churchill on Hudson Bay, he added, "It's the real tundra, the true sub-Arctic and, the remarkable thing about it is that you can get there by train."

Arthur Fuller was a retired, accomplished museum taxidermist and the one individual perhaps most responsible for getting me interested in the Arctic. He had worked for the Cleveland Museum of Natural History and had made many collecting trips to the Churchill area. He had retired to a small farm on Virginia's eastern shore but continued to accept bird and mammal mounting assignments in a small way. I became acquainted with him when I worked as a biologist for the Virginia Commission of Game and Inland Fisheries and persuaded him to start a collection of bird and mammal mounts for us, a task he finally undertook and performed amazingly well.

Some years later I was traveling the continent on a doctoral research assignment and found myself one mid-July in Winnipeg at the Canadian National Railway ticket window.

"I suppose you want a berth?" the ticket agent asked. "You know it's two days and nights to Churchill." I nodded and settled for an upper. It was a trip I shall never forget—dressing and undressing in cramped quarters, trying to make out with a swinging net full of clothes, a windowless bed from which one soon learns all the ways and sounds of the train intimately.

I recall that the puffing train rolled out of the station on schedule and began a slow, jostling, frequently-stopping journey northward. Yet I never enjoyed a more fascinating rail trip in my life.

For several hours the scenery was one of passing prairie lands, lakes, evergreen forests, and what Canadians call *bush*. All through Canada the reference *bush* is heard frequently—farmers do not

The beginning of the taiga forest near Churchill.

clear the forests for agriculture, they clear the *bush;* trappers go *into the bush;* local pilots are *bush pilots.* Our train then was heading for the northern *bush.*

One soon learns too that the rail lines up here are life and blood to the north country. People live along the railroad and look to it for transportation and a means of communication. As you go farther and farther north this dependence on the train becomes more pronounced. The stops are frequent—the passengers get out and walk around, there is a friendly exchange of greetings between travelers and the natives, mostly Indians, then the train whistles and everyone climbs aboard again and the train moves on. It is kind of fun.

The scenery doesn't change much until the morning of the second day when, well past the town of The Pas, the country definitely takes on a wild northern character. This is the beginning of the so-called taiga, that interesting transition zone, or ecotone, where the solid boreal forest begins to dwarf and yield to an open kind of landscape that I have since learned has been unfortunately labeled as the *Barrens,* which is the true tundra. At first you only get a peek of this open land here and there, but by afternoon you begin to cross great stretches of it.

When the train finally pulls into Churchill it is very early in the morning and the settlement looks bleak and desolate. In the distance you can see the Churchill River, the huge grain elevators —which seem out of place in this country—and the rocky escarpment bordering Hudson Bay. Indeed, you sense this place as another world.

Churchill is definitely heavy jacket or parka country. The morning temperatures are in their thirties and forties and the afternoons in their fifties. The air has a definite Arctic chill to it, and the wind sweeping inland from Hudson Bay, still locked in much ice, is penetrating.

The walking distance from the train station to a place called Churchill Point is a good two miles or what the natives say "a bit of a hike." And indeed it was. Down along the river's edge the hiking was all over rocks; some were huge and smooth and polished as tumbled gems, others formed into ledges twisting and flowing in great convolutions in every direction. Churchill Point is where the exposed massive rock, which the geologists call the Canadian Shield, meets the mouth of the Churchill River and Hudson Bay. It's a natural point of rock to visit, only the going is all

The exposed Canadian Shield surrounding southern Hudson Bay.

up and down over boulders, across ledges, and over great rocks. When I finally reached the point I got the feeling that this was surely the beginning of the Arctic—a cold fearsome place where raw elements rule yet exciting and thrilling. You quickly get the feeling that you want to explore and there isn't enough time for everything.

A few days of romping around these rocks and over the desolate landscape and one feels like a new person. Nowhere does the air seem fresher or the breezes more stimulating. And it seems that so much oxygen goes into one's system here that sleep at night is no problem. Never have I slept better in any strange country than at Churchill, in this isolated land of the southern sub-Arctic fringe.

The taiga around this part of Hudson Bay is full of surprises. After a good night's rain the tundra suddenly awakens. Wildflowers, small and delicate, appear everywhere, and over this floral carpet flutter and fly and chirp many birds. Though it is July the birds seem to herald the beginning of a new season. The golden plover is especially an interesting bird of these parts and nesting pairs are frequently seen. So are the snow bunting, longspur, and many forms of sparrows. Here and there stately Canada geese gather in small flocks, wary but not nervous like they are in the cornfields of Maryland or Virginia.

Still further back in the taiga, away from the shores of Hudson Bay, the tundra is interspersed with ridges and lowlands. Here stretch the open prairies marred by clumps of spruce islands. The limbs of all of the trees are twisted and torn and flow in the same direction—away from the almost perpetual North Wind. As you tread through this forsaken land, between the ridges of rock and the lowlands, filled with soggy marsh grass, you see deep furrows across the land and walking in them is suddenly made easy. They are

The dwindling taiga near Churchill.

trails made by caribou and they are old and worn deep through many years of use. There are large hoof prints in the baked mud of some of the trails and you wonder how many weeks it's been since the animals passed through the area.

Back in town there is occasional talk of caribou, how the great herds range north, and how easy it is to shoot them. But now the talk is mostly about the offshore ice, when it will disappear, and how soon the ships will come in.

One leaves Churchill after a much too brief initial visit, feeling somewhat like a big boy with altogether too small an ice cream cone. You want more and you vow, someday, to return and get it.

On my way back to Winnipeg I met a man who kept telling me about James Bay, the lower loop basin of Hudson Bay, and what a great place this area was to see.

The author examines a dwarf spruce tree on the tundra. *Courtesy Robert F. Holmes, National Audubon Society.*

Byron L. Ashbaugh of the National Audubon Society overlooks the tundra near Churchill.

"You must go there, too," he said. "It's different but still the sub-Arctic. I especially like the waterfowl there. Great place for geese. White ones. They call them snows. They breed there, but many go further north."

"Yes, I know," I said, "they go to the country called 'beyond the north wind.' "

Some years after my first visit to Churchill I returned to this sub-Arctic point for more extensive explorations. I wanted to study and photograph the many different habitats that are so richly represented here.

One evening I went out on the carpeted Barrens and there for the first time watched the phalarope twirling in the lakelet. I followed the bird to another pond and there spotted more of these sandpipers. I also saw some old squaw ducks, a sora, and some yellow rail. I was with two companions, Byron L. Ashbaugh and Robert F. Holmes, both of the National Audubon Society, and with a rented car we toured much of the taiga country. In one wet area we discovered a thick carpet of *Cladonia* lichen, or caribou moss, and photographed it. It grew lush and thick and, with bog rosemary and other low heath plants, was an exciting habitat to study.

Another evening the lure to visit Churchill Point was compelling and we took to the rocks once again. It was hand-purple cold and an icy wind was whipping out of the northeast, sweeping over the bay. With it in gusts came biting sleet and snow, glazing over the boulders and covering the whole rocky point with a mantle of white. The sun had disappeared for days and a remorseless gloom hung over this strange point.

Breaking the long, curving shore of Hudson Bay a wide,

Caribou moss, a lichen, an important food of the caribou in the taiga.

A common flowering plant on the tundra is the Arctic avens.

greenish-white line marked the mouth of the Churchill River. The river was open but for miles carried cakes of ice and bits of frozen silt only to intermingle with the colder, more ice-choked waters of the bay. In places where the waters joined, the floes caked up and caused tortured ridges to form. Great five-foot-thick platforms of ice formed, piled one upon the other. The ice had come floating down the river from still-cold ice fields many miles away. Embedded in the cakes of ice were rocks and pebbles and fragments of limestone shale. In a recent flood, brought on by a recent thaw, the waters had scoured the riverbanks far up in the taiga and carried much silt for miles to the brackish waters of the bay. Beyond where the ice floes piled up and ice ridges formed, the bay was an endless expanse of ice as far as the eye could see. Suddenly, on the thrust of a great gust of North Wind, a tumultuous sound boomed across the earth and almost instantly a blue streak broke full length across the frozen bay. The early summer's break-up of sea ice had begun on Hudson Bay.

Hudson Bay ice breakup near Churchill.

Very soon, perhaps a few days, maybe as much as a week, the river and the bay would be alive with whitefish and the white ghosts of the Arctic waters would come in. Then every day on the incoming tide, the Eskimos would study the river and the wind, check their canoes and motors in preparation for the excitement to come.

Then one night the wind shifts and at last the break-up is in full swing. In the dawn's early chill all the ice is floating out to sea. Almost instantly, the river has come alive with wallowing, ivory-colored forms, the beluga white whales, and the season for hunting them is on.

The manner of the hunter and the hunted in these waters is simple enough. An Eskimo, rifle in hand, takes to a large canoe equipped with a motor, harpoon, rope, and barrel and streaks out into the middle of the river. There he waits, motor idling, harpoon ready, scanning the water for the white head and back of a beluga to surface. When one shows up he gives chase. The beluga senses danger and submerges quickly and heads upstream. But the hunter knows the whale's speed, judges the time it will "blow" for air again and closes in. Slowly the chase narrows down the distance. Finally, when the canoe and beluga are in close range, the hunter throws the harpoon. Out flows the rope, ten, twenty, forty feet and then the orange-colored barrel. The beluga's neck is pierced and it puts on a burst of speed. But it must surface again for air, when the Eskimo delivers the *coup de grace* with several shots from his rifle. Thereafter it is merely a long wait, a slow death for the white ghost, when belly up it floats, twelve full feet of it, on the surface. Now begins the arduous, slow, and often dangerous tow to the small whale factory on the river's shore. The price at the factory is $1.25 per foot of whale.

One noon hour down at the river's edge I came upon a member of the Royal Canadian Mounted Police who was preparing to take a

Eskimo shacks near Churchill, Manitoba.

small party—two women, a man, and a boy—across the river to
Fort Churchill. I engaged him in conversation and took a few pictures.

"Would you like to come along?" he said. "It's a bit windy and
rough but we should make it. Might see some belugas on the
way."

I thought about the weather and big water, but seeing the size of
the war canoe, its motor, and ample life jackets, I said, "Yes."

For a few minutes the going was sensible enough but soon we
began meeting rough water, a swirling current, and larger and
larger whitecaps. Soon we were riding a dangerous sea and all of
us began to get nervous. Soon we found ourselves in the mouth of
the treacherous Churchill River with the awesome waters of Hudson Bay piling in all around us. Icy spray poured over us and the
canoe bucked and tossed and crashed. It seemed suicidal to progress any further and I wanted to tell the Mountie to turn around.
Just then a large white shadow surfaced nearby and spouted spray
over us. It held itself half exposed for several seconds and you
could see its eye clearly. It seemed to be giving us a warning as if
to say, "You fools, turn back. I'm in my element but you are
not." Then it went down. It was a great sight for a moment but
there was no time to appreciate it.

"Yes, it's just too rough, folks," said the Mountie. "We'll turn
around. Anyway, you got a good close-up of a white whale."

The sergeant's voice was calm but it was obvious that he was
alarmed. Slowly, cautiously, he maneuvered the craft around,
while all of us, breathless and cold and frozen, held on for dear
life. Finally we edged out of the dangerous eddies and began plowing toward the calmer waters of the shore. When we reached the
gravel bank and set foot on solid earth at last, I felt immensely
relieved. Never had I been this near to a sea disaster in my life.

"Close, wasn't it!" I remarked to the sergeant.

He just beamed for a moment but his ruddy complexion had
turned white and he was trembling as he helped us out of the craft.
Then I realized how great had been our danger. All that needed to
happen was for a big wave to hit us broadside and we would have
been spilled into the water—water just above the freezing point is
an immense shock to the human system. So paralyzing would the
immersion have been that even with life jackets and good swimming ability, none of us would have been able to last longer than a
few minutes.

The beluga is a true whale, a mammal, but being small, one should know how it fits in with the mammal groups called porpoises and dolphins.

Dolphins, porpoises, killer whales, blackfish, white whales, narwhales, and others all belong to the dolphin family. They are really small whales. Like the rest of the toothed whales, the belugas have a single blowhole in their foreheads. Most of these dolphins are from five to fourteen feet long, but some species may run up to thirty feet in length. One can distinguish them from the other whales by their smaller size.

The porpoises and dolphins are among the smaller cetaceans. In size they range from five to fourteen feet, but included in this family are several "whales," the white whale or beluga, the killer whale, and the narwhale that may be up to thirty feet long.

With the exception of the black finless porpoise, white whale, and narwhale, all have dorsal fins. Those of the dolphins curve backward at a rackish angle; the porpoises' and the killers' are more triangular in shape. The common dolphins are recognized by their long jaws, forming "beaks," which the rest of the family do not have.

The lives of dolphins, such as the beluga white whale, are much the same as the larger whales. But there are some outstanding differences.

According to Victor Cahalane, the big whales usually prefer their own company or a few boon companions at the most, while the dolphins surround themselves with friends. As many as eight hundred white whales have been seen swimming together up the St. Lawrence River.

On occasions, North American dolphins may take excursions up rivers farther than whales ever venture. At least one school of dolphins ascended the Hudson River as far as Poughkeepsie. Dead common dolphins have been found in the Hudson at Highland, seventy-three miles north of New York Harbor, and at Van Wies Point, one hundred and forty-five miles above New York.

While the largest of the dolphin family are sometimes sought for their oil, most of the group are regarded as too small for commercial "whaling." At one time, however, a fishery for the common bottle-nosed dolphin was carried on at Cape Hatteras. They were netted in some numbers, 1,268 being caught during one winter. The white beluga, however, is still pursued to some extent in the north.

The common porpoise, which weighs from one hundred to one hundred and twenty pounds, was once used extensively for food. During medieval times, it was considered a royal dish. In the days when men were men, strong-smelling fat meat was not objectionable.*

The last evening before our departure from Churchill, we went down to the point again to watch the belugas. The sub-Arctic evening glow was still sufficient in light to take pictures. We set up our cameras and gasped.

"There must be a dozen out there," Byron said through a throat obviously dry and parched. He was angling his camera for the best shots. "Yes," he said, trembling a bit, "what I wouldn't give to be out there right now. . .among them. . .in a boat, eyeball to eyeball."

The whales were surfacing, one after another, fifteen visible at one time. Then more appeared. In a few minutes still more showed themselves. Soon the river was alive with myriads of surfacing shiny white forms—a hundred belugas streaming up the Churchill River.

We took pictures but trembled in doing so. The white ghosts of the sub-Arctic country had us in a spell.

*Victor H., Cahalane, *Mammals of North America* (New York: Macmillan Co., 1961).

4
Call of the Sub-Arctic Wilderness

The Arctic is not all ice and snow, not all treeless tundra. Along its sub-Arctic fringe are circumpolar forests, half dense and closed, half sparse and open, with large areas still wild and abounding with animal life.

In North America this so-called big country of the evergreens, the *Hudsonian* wilderness, is a region of vast boreal trees stretching from Newfoundland to the Yukon Territory and on into central and southern Alaska, five thousand miles long and a thousand miles wide—the finest stand of native spruce and fir in the world.

The closed Hudsonian is the dark green world of the marten, an inquisitive arboreal weasel that is sleek and beautiful, and its larger cousin, the fleet-footed fisher, the handsome cat of the tall timber. Both are agile creatures and carry the most precious and elegant furs in the animal kingdom, excelling in beauty and texture even that of the ermine.

The wilderness of the Hudsonian is also the home of large animals, like the huge antlered "king of the muskegs," the moose. It is the natural realm of the woodland caribou and the last retreat of the freedom-loving timber wolf. It is the land of strong-hearted men, trappers, woodsmen, prospectors, and hunters, men who can take fierce cold and much whiskey and who enjoy loneliness.

One sleeting day while walking a narrow path far back in this wilderness I was startled suddenly by the figure of a bearded man in the trail. The encounter froze me in my tracks like a statue. I held still for a moment until the meeting made sense, then extended a friendly greeting. The man was a French-Canadian and was headed for the heavy bush, he said, for the purpose of curing his whiskey habit.

"Oh, yes, I take *leethle* along, but when it goes I sober up. And for *goot*." It was plain that he loved the wilderness and believed in its great therapeutic powers.

"But Jean," I said, "how do you stand the long winters, without any company and without women."

"Ah, wimmin, my friend," he came back, "they is wonderful. But man must make a living and the wilderness, she calls."

The Hudsonian forest country in its southern range is a tight or closed wilderness. It is thick and difficult to penetrate and one must stay clear of the muskegs if he is to move about. This means keeping to old logging trails or granite ridges where natural openings occur. In the northern forest range, however, the country gradually opens up. The spruce and fir and aspen trees are smaller, more sparse, and the forests take the characteristics of the true taiga. It is this open boreal forest that forms the greater part of the sub-Arctic wilderness, perhaps the wildest, most primeval of its kind remaining in the world today. A sojourn into this kind of far northland where there are no roads, no reminders of civilization, can be a unique experience.

I was lured into just this kind of a place one fall in the hope of seeing snow geese. The geese were said to be gathering on the taiga flats around James Bay, but the going promised to be so tough that my companions and I settled for the central Spanish Lakes country a hundred miles to the south. We had driven our cars as far as the roads would take us in northern Ontario and then at Capreol changed to a train. From this northern outpost the Canadian National took us several hundred more miles north to a certain spot where a lone cabin stood along the railroad tracks. When the train came to a halt and we seemed literally to be dumped off, Ken Ludlam, one of the genial souls in our party, just stood there outside the steaming train, bundled in a huge parka, and mused: "Gentlemen, I gather, we have come to the sub-Arctic wilderness and Dave Weiner has lured us here to charter a new Northwest Passage. . .or to start another Gold Rush."

The cabin belonged to Dave and the rumor was that he had purchased it through some special deal, sight unseen because it was

Hunting party in the sub-Arctic James Bay country.

in the Timmins area and in the heart of fabulous moose country.

There were eight of us in the party and when we descended, guns dangling from shoulders, upon Dave's cabin and a small shack nearby, we indeed looked the part of a fearsome group of toughs from a city. Sedg Watson of our gang was a forest ranger from Virginia's George Washington National Forest and chuckled frequently in his throat as reference to the Hilton and Waldorf were made. This was his kind of country, he loved and showed it. I had hand-picked Sedg to join us because of his intimate knowledge of the wilderness, having worked a long time in the Maine woods and other forest areas. We both graduated together from the New York State Ranger School, in the Adirondacks, and knew each other well. Somehow, with Sedg along, we couldn't lose.

Sedg always said that the wilderness had a special spirit and beauty all its own and if one wanted to really know it, he would have to live in it awhile.

For a whole week we fanned out into the bush country, usually in pairs, sometimes alone, but saw no moose. There were plenty of tracks in the snow, many as large as those of a huge ox, but none of us saw even the faintest glimpse of a moose. Some new strategy apparently was in order.

One morning I decided to really see this wild land and set out alone for the remote area. Sedg surmised that the big antlered plodders were feeding in the deepest part of the Spanish River country and if we were to find any, this is where we would have to go. I checked a map, grabbed a bagged lunch, and took off. Within an hour or so I found myself in an area full of glacial lakes, beaver dams, and rolling hills. Step by step the country gained in a special kind of wilderness flavor, a deep spirit of aloneness and tranquility, and I relished it. Such unbelievable solitude I had not quite tasted before.

All morning long I followed huge tracks in the snow, plowing into one muskeg and out another, out into openings sprinkled with birch and alders, and into ravines and across windswept eskers. At one point I found myself in an impenetrable black spruce thicket and wondered how a large moose with rocking-chairlike antlers could ever get through it. The hours ticked by. Now my map and compass told me I was getting deeper and deeper into unchartered country. Would a bull moose ever show? Would any large animal ever come into view? True, this was a vast country and there was lots of hiding room, yet with so many tracks something should show up. On the tracks went and finally the noon hour arrived. I stopped beside an old moss covered log, brushed away the snow, and sat down. There was a deep pervasive silence in the forest. A friendly black-capped chickadee flittered from limb to limb in a balsam tree, eyeing me carefully, wondering, I suspect, what this strange creature was doing up here in his wild wilderness. I spoke softly to the bird and then made a peculiar noise by sucking air across the back of my hand, which normally attracts small birds. The trick worked. The little feathered fellow displayed much inquisitiveness and at one point came almost to my outstretched hand. It kept up its friendly *chic. . .dee. . .dee* and finally flew off for the deeper woods.

As I was finishing my last sandwich a red squirrel chattered high in a distant spruce. Nearby, but invisible, I could hear a sapsucker working over a dead tree. A chilly north wind now began to whisper gently, almost musically, through the tall evergreens and I was deeply moved by it all. This was real Thoreau wilderness, supreme solitude. The great wilderness was speaking. I felt very much alone but not lonely. There is a difference.

The feeling brings to mind the words of a great man, John Stuart Mill, who in 1848 described the spirit of solitude better than any man I know.

"A population may be too crowded," Mill said, "though all be amply supplied with food and raiment. It is not good for man to be kept perforce at all times in the presence of his species. A world from which solitude is extirpated is a very poor deal. Solitude, in the sense of being often alone, is essential to any depth of meditation or of character; and solitude in the presence of natural beauty and grandeur is the cradle of thoughts and aspirations which are not only good for the individual, but which society could ill do without. Nor is there much satisfaction in contemplating the world with nothing left to the spontaneous activity of nature; with every road of land brought into cultivation which is capable of growing food for human beings; every flowery waste or natural pasture ploughed up, all quadrupeds or birds which are not domesticated for man's use exterminated as his rivals for food, every hedgerow or superfluous tree rooted out, and scarcely a place left where a wild shrub or flower could grow without being eradicated as a weed in the name of improved agriculture."

I reflected at length on the words of Mill when a mental flash told me it was time to stir. I had sojourned now some eight or ten miles and unless I saw a moose soon, it would be time to turn back. But the lure of the wilderness is subtle and strong and urges one on. There is a thirst to it that is unquenchable. And, it is a kind of drinking which one should partake of more often. Once more I arose and took to the trail.

When two o'clock had come and passed away and no moose had revealed itself, I began to wonder. What if I should be lost? No, there was the compass. The tracks led on. When the sun finally dipped to the treetops, I stopped, thought a thousand thoughts, squinted once more at the sinking sun, and turned around to retracing my footprints back through the snow. The disappointment was deep but there was hope I might still see my moose on the back trail.

Reaching the first of the glaciated lakes, the one I considered as the midway point back to camp, the day was approaching twilight. It was here in the heart of the great Canadian wilderness where I received my first full baptism of spirit of this big country. It came in the form of a wild voice out of a snow-covered valley. Out from beyond a distant lake it came, a long, drawn out cry, an awesome sound that sent shockwaves down my spine. My heart rose up into my neck.

The eerie sound froze me in the snow. I listened, breathlessly, heart throbbing enormous beats in my neck. In a short suspenseful minute it came again, a lonesome *ooo. . .ooo, ooo. . .ooo, uh, uh,* followed by a *yip, yip,* like a wailing dog in a far-off clenching steel trap. The howl seemed to come from a blanket of heavy timber about a half mile away and ended in an echo down the valley. Shivering, I clamped my jaws and moved on. The voice was familiar. I know enough about the biology of the wolf not to be mentally afraid. Studies had told me of no authentic record where a human had ever been attacked or killed by a wolf in North America—unprovoked, unmolested. But what is provocation? Soon, a second voice joined the first, then a third, then a fourth. Footsteps quickening, I hastened on, eyes wide open, scanning all corners of the darkening trail. Now the stars began to twinkle. It was going to be a clear, cold night.

At a high point on a ridge, near a beaver pond, I paused to catch my breath, and listened. The world suddenly went silent. Incredible quiet held the wilderness in a mighty grip. No wind, no breeze, just cavelike stillness was the night. Now the trail ahead would lead through solid black timber all the way to camp, a distance of some four miles. That was a long way and the air was chilling. A slight breeze commenced again. Again, I took another long, deep breath, cupped my ear to the North Wind and listened. There came the faint gurgling of water through the beaver dam and it was comforting. It was the only sound in the darkness.

Suddenly, uncomfortably close this time, a lone wolf once more began his songfest. Then in a moment, from another ridge, came a second howl. Then another. Then the voices of a small group all joined together. . .all howling, each in a separate voice, each in a different area, each some distance apart, now wailing, now yipping, now yelping. From many directions there arose a whole medley of wild voices, some high, some low, some just howls and barks. A few came on long and lengthening and filled the air in a wide arc around the lake, *ah. . .ooo. . .ooo. . .oooo. . .oooo!* Chilled, leg muscles trembling, I stood there silently in the dark, wondering. Once more the assurance came that timber wolves never attack a human being. But, somehow, the thought at the moment held little comfort. Mentally, I was unafraid. Physically, my body was reacting normally. I clutched my 30-06 tightly, tilted back my cap and, with renewed courage, took to the night again.

Suddenly the wolf serenade came to an abrupt halt. For the third time I was forced to halt, to listen. It was a peculiar feeling, one moment something telling you to move on, then another to wait, to hear the music. But the trembling—I felt almost ashamed. But a man doesn't hear a wolf symphony very often, so why not take advantage of it and listen? Why not enjoy it? These and other thoughts preoccupied my attention when, directly below, from the deepest and closest timber yet, came a voice that made my heart sink. On a breath of haunted wind it came, rising melodiously, pitched low at first, then rising clearly higher and higher—a steady sad cry, holding long and clear and even, then lowering slightly in intensity, and finally ending in notes so hushed, so muted that my ears could barely catch them—a wolf crying out the beauty of the night, singing a love song as no human could sing, pouring out a wild deep-felt yearning to another lonesome wolf to come join him to share his company. Over and over the song of the wolf filled the night until, at last, from somewhere in the black recesses of the night, came an answering call. Then there followed a strange performance, a duet. As if howling through some megaphone, one by one, the two love-starved creatures began to answer one another. Closer and closer the voices came until at last their calls seemed to merge into one. Then a whole chorus of voices rose from other wolves, as if singing a hallelujah to the meeting that had taken place.

How many voices? As best as I was able to judge there were fourteen wolves in that sing around the lake. And while they seemed a reasonable distance away, their calls in the stillness of the night and the accoustical quality of the lake, made them sound very close.

After the two wolves met and were serenaded by several others the main pack evidently broke up into several groups and started hunting again. A hunting wolf does not really howl but emits a kind of high-pitched, staccatolike yapping, very much like an excited dog when he hits a hot game trail. Satisfied they were after hares and that the main symphony was over, I took to the fast-darkening trail with renewed vigor and courage.

When I finally reached the cabin, hours later, I thought about

Wolf in snow. *Courtesy Arthur Ambler, National Audubon Society.*

my day. I had seen no moose but I had been thrilled by the elements of a great wilderness. After dinner my companions, who
also went mooseless, and I went out on the cabin porch to listen.
The wolves were still at it but their calls were barely audible.
Slowly, one by one, their howls grew fainter and further apart,
suggesting that the revelry of wolf music, for one night at least,
was over.

During the night a fresh snowfall came and covered the evergreen wilderness with six inches of fluffy white loveliness. I was up
stirring around soon after sun-up and after dressing went outside to
get some water from a nearby spring. Along the path not fifty
yards from the cabin I came upon the fresh imprints of one of our
revelers of the night. The tracks were immense. I could hardly believe my eyes. I broke sticks from an alder bush to measure their
length and width. On an old yardstick in the cabin they measured 6
by 4½ inches. Several days later Sedg and I stopped to check one

of these great animals as he flashed by in a thicket. We were prepared unfortunately for geese on a small open peninsula and Sedg
threw a load of shot at this wolf but missed.

The gray wolf in this taiga land is unbelievably big. The total
length of these wolves range from fifty-five to sixty-seven inches,
plus a tail of twelve to nineteen inches. Their height at the shoulder
runs from twenty-six to twenty-eight inches and more. Their weight
varies from seventy to 180 pounds. Wolves seem to show a tremendous variation in color but the average appears very much like
a big German shepherd dog. From this form, the animals seem to
vary from the almost white coat found in Alaska to the black phase
sometimes seen in the wild. The head of the wolf is distinctive: a
broad face with a wide but short nose and blazing eyes. The eyes
sometimes appear straw colored and always have round pupils. The
ears are short and round, and much more like a dog's than a

An Arctic wolf pup.

coyote's. The feet of the timber wolf, in keeping with the rest of the body, seem very large, which always is amazing to me. The front feet have five toes, as is usual with canines, the first toe or *thumb* does not touch the ground. The hind foot has but four toes.

Wolves are known to have a high reproduction rate. Each year the single litter may consist of from three to four pups to as many as twelve. The average, however, is said to be from six to eight.

The wolf's association with man, of course, is older than recorded history. When man first gained control over other mammals, it was the wolf that somehow became a dog. As man's partner in the chase, it helped him to become the one superior animal that today is capable of exterminating all wildlife. Today man has come close to doing just that and the wolf is now an endangered species. Only a few thousand of these magnificent animals remain in the United States, mostly in Minnesota. Before long the species probably will become extinct in continental United States, unless stern conservation measures are taken. Fortunately, large numbers of wolves still persist in Alaska and Canada and should remain there for many years.

Much of man's antipathy for wolves comes from literature. Who, as a child, has not thrilled to the danger that surrounded Little Red Riding Hood, and rejoiced at the ultimate end of the archvillain? Long before animated cartooning took over nursery rhymes, children's books were well thumbmarked at the page where the "big bad wolf huffed and puffed and blew the house down." To "keep the wolf from the door" is an expression as full of meaning today as it was in the fifteenth century when the animal became extinct in England. The wolf has always been a symbol of ruthlessness. The genus *Lupinus* (Latin: wolf), a beautiful group of plants of the pea family, is so called because early botanists thought it robbed the soil. The "wolf" so often encountered at house parties is included in this class. None of these characterizations gives a good impression, and all are indicative of man's feeling toward the wolf. It is most unfortunate that man so often condemns anything that interferes with his own economic progress. Nature has a place for the wolf, a specialized task for which it is admirably adapted. The role of the wolf in the north country is biologically useful and vital.

In the days before the white man, bison roamed the western plains in great herds that were constantly followed by packs of wolves and coyotes. As long as the bison remained close together they were relatively safe, but woe to the sick or weak that lagged behind. These were quickly pulled down, and when the wolves had eaten the choicest portions, the coyotes and vultures moved in for the rest. When the white man exterminated the bison, the wolves' host was gone and they turned to the logical substitute, the whie man's cattle. This could have but one result. In the predator control campaign that followed, a wedge was driven through the wolf population, leaving various groups isolated. This began a serious wolf decline. Moreover, during the extermination program, a terribly abominable practice was begun, using a violent poison as a killer. The behavior of the wolf was affected to a considerable extent as a result.

Accounts of early travelers stress the easy familiarity with which the gray wolf accepted their presence. When a wayfarer shot a bison, the wolf sat down within easy range and waited until the choicest cuts had been taken away. It then moved in for its share. Since that time the wolf has become one of the most wary and cunning of our wild creatures. Gifted with keen intelligence, it has learned that only by complete isolation can it escape the methods devised for its destruction. To this end, it has moved into the more inaccessible places in the mountains and into the northern boreal forests, especially northern Ontario and the prairie provinces, into British Columbia and the Yukon and Northwest Territories.

The sprawling Hudsonian wilderness is a priceless outdoor heritage to Americans. Economically, of course, this enormous forest empire possesses great wealth. There is the temptation to exploit it to the full. Yet the recreational, esthetic, and spiritual values present in the long run seem of greater worth. Surely segments of this fascinating natural world need to be preserved, for if we do not, there will be no marten, no moose, no timber wolves in the future. And when these are gone, America and its people will have lost a remarkable aspect of its wild heritage.

5

On the Trail of the Wandering Tuk-tu

"We have operations going on in the summer in the eastern as well as the central Arctic," wrote Dr. A. Munro, chief of the Canadian Wildlife Service, "and while both regions are interesting, the central Arctic is where you will most likely see waterfowl and big game." He spoke of the Thelon country in the Northwest Territories as being the most promising area, and he would put me in touch with the regional and local officials.

The information was exciting. Yes, I would start making arrangements early and go in July to the Far North where the tundra opens wide and much wildlife *might* be seen.

It was January when I contacted Dr. Munro, and it was good that it was, for it takes months of arrangements for a loner to get into the remote Arctic. My final contact man was Robert A. Ruttan, an experienced wildlife biologist, who was making plans to tag caribou again—his fourth summer—on the Arctic Barrens.

Bob Ruttan and I soon had quite a correspondence going, clearing up such details as how to get to our rendezvous point, equipment, clothing, food, sleeping gear, and so on. His last letter said something about bringing in some "fresh steaks and lettuce" from my final jump-off point in northern Saskatchewan.

"Lettuce, in the Arctic," I thought in a bit of puzzlement. . .well, I would try.

In mid-July I flew to Edmonton, Alberta, visited a few days with relatives, and then made preparations to leave for the North.

On July 20 a series of power-packed events began to cause me much anxiety. The tenseness of preparing for a trip into wild country had occupied my full attention for three days and the pressure now really began to build up. Edmonton is the main jump-off point for aerial trips into the Arctic region and one can feel the spirit of the North rising. You can enter the vast no-man's-land of the Canadian Arctic through several avenues: through Labrador, or the west coast of Hudson Bay, principally with Churchill as a base, or by way of Yellowknife on Great Slave Lake, or by Edmonton to the northeast. Modern, sprawling Edmonton, capital of Alberta, is still the popular main gateway to the central Arctic.

The traveler soons finds in this country that airlines have their delays and old vintage C-3s, the planes of World War II fame, have their troubles. My particular scheduled plane had its problems, a faulty magneto. But it was soon replaced, and after an hour of waiting, a dozen passengers and I were up and over Edmonton and heading north. Our destination was Uranium City, on Lake Athabasca, in northern Saskatchewan, with a stopover at Fort McMurray.

In the early days of sailing vessels and steam barges the six-hundred-mile stretch between Edmonton and Athabasca was the scene of feverish summer activity—overland transport and barge trips down rivers and across lakes from Fort McMurray to mighty Lake Athabasca. Now most light freight and practically all passenger service is carried by aircraft.

The country between Fort Murray and Lake Athabasca is still very wild. The vegetation is chiefly white spruce and fir and aspen with scattered patches of birch and willow. It is rolling, moderately rough terrain with lakes so green-blue as to seem unreal. This is the region of the *tree country* where the moose makes its perpetual home and where the Barren Ground caribou come and spread out in the winter.

Our plane was an interesting aircraft. On one side all the seats had been taken out to provide for air freight. The other side had the conventional seats, enough to accomodate fourteen passengers. A single stewardess served coffee and kept a watchful eye on the lashed-down crates, cartons, and gasoline (*petrol* in Canada) drums. Were it not for petrol to power planes and boats and heat cookstoves, it is doubtful if the northern bush and the Arctic beyond could sustain humans.

The region around Lake Athabasca is an answer to an outdoorsman's dream—be he fisherman, hunter, canoeist, or naturalist. Perhaps nowhere in North America is the combination of rivers, evergreen forests, and lakes more pronounced and all in such a superb wilderness setting. Much of the land is untouched by axe, saw, and fire. Great sections of northern Alberta, Saskatchewan, and Manitoba are roadless and still personify the real wilderness.

Uranium City is really not a city in the traditional sense. It is a frontier town, much like the character of other outposts like Yellowknife and Forth Smith in the Northwest Territories and Whitehorse in the Yukon Territory. The town is set down several miles from Lake Athabasca, amid rough outcroppings of granite and sandstone but adorned on all sides by fir and spruce and aspen. It is a dry, dusty place, with some stores, cottages, a few garages, a movie house, a couple of mediocre cafes and a combination, hotel-bar and restaurant. A two-storied headquarters of the Royal Canadian Mounted Police (R.C.M.P., built of shining white clapboard, is the neatest building in town. Like all Royal Canadian Mounted Police posts in the north country, it is the eyes and ears of much that happens in its district—and some of the districts run as much as one hundred thousand square miles in size.

I quickly gathered that the town was definitely on the downgrade since the discovery of new and more accessible sources of uranium came into being in other parts of Canada and the United States.

I spent three days in Uranium City, walking around its gravelly streets and perimeter in an effort to learn what I could about it. To my surprise some of the houses and shacks had small vegetable gardens, the chief product being potatoes. Apparently the long sun-lit days are good for most root vegetables. Many forms of vegetables are grown right to the edge of the Arctic Circle further west in the MacKenzie region and in Alaska.

The hotel where I stayed was nice and clean and reasonably modern, attesting to the fact that the town was a booming place a decade back when the uranium mine was operating full blast and the town boasted of nearly ten thousand residents. Now the population was down to a mere two thousand, although even this seemed high from all outward appearances.

There is no doubt that Uranium City is a jump-off point for the great wild country to the north. Everything suggests it—the talk of the natives, half of whom appear to be Indians of the Cree and

Chipewyan breed, a dark-skinned variety with high cheekbones and straight, jet-black hair and mostly speaking broken English. At first they appear suspicious and seem unfriendly to outsiders. In the evening when the mine lets out there are more people in town and the street corner around the restaurant is a favorite gathering and gossipping point. The talk is mostly about fishing and hunting and the Barrens of the north.

In the Hudson's Bay Company store on the hill there is more of that atmosphere of frontierland—foodstuffs and general supplies for campers, prospectors, and fishermen. Prices are high because everything must be airfreighted in from Edmonton or barged up from Fort McMurray.

To my dismay two items of my vital equipment were not to be found in town. One was a pair of hip boots or waders, the other an essential bit of protection against mosquitoes, a head net and sleeping bar. I reported this to Jean Buck, the dispatcher at the McMurray Airlines, who was my liaison official. Jean acted as a point of contact with the outside world and Bob Ruttan, my would-be host on the Arctic Barrens. She said she would try to find me some boots but that as for the other items, I would have to improvise or go without. Fortunately I located some wide cheesecloth at the H. B. store, bought needles and thread, and decided to improvise my own head net and sleeping bar. I chided myself that I should have brought all these things with me or purchased them in Edmonton. I was so provoked over this predicament that I was downright uneasy and wakeful at night. The lesson learned was simple: never to depend on final outfitting at your jump-off point. Local stores just might not have the items you need.

As it did not get dark until after ten o'clock I had time to putter about in my room as well as spend an hour or so in the restaurant. I went to the bar not so much to drink beer, which is about all that was permitted to be sold here, but to observe the people in it. There were only about a dozen persons there, sitting around tables in dimly lit booths, plus a single, busy young waiter trying to serve everybody. About half of the group were women, mostly Indians, and I could overhear hard language and filthy talk. One middle-aged, hard-looking squaw kept coming in and out of the bar, first talking with this Indian and then with a white man, obviously trying to arouse interest. But she found no takers. I saw no big, hardy characters, like the one I came in contact with in Whitehorse some years back. It was on a Saturday evening. I recall I went into this

particular bar, ordered a beer and casually began sipping away
when a great man, with a big moustache walked in and announced,
"I'm the toughest S.O.B. in the Yukon and I can lick any bastard
in Whitehorse. Do I have a taker?"

At this point, sensing there was going to be trouble, I finished
my beer and unobtrusively left the bar and went to my hotel. I
knew the kind of recreation some of these places have on weekends
and wanted no part of it.

Next morning I was having Sunday breakfast in the Whitehorse
cafe and, lo and behold, who comes into the cafe but this same
tough, Saturday night giant. One eye was swollen shut and three
huge adhesive tapes were draped tight over his reddened cheek.

"Well, what in the world happened to you, my friend?" I asked
good naturedly.

The man sat down on a stool and glared out at me through the
remaining bloodshot eye, then barked, "Me! Why, nothin! You
should see the other seven bastards I got mixed up with."

In another twenty-four hours Jean Buck alerted me and gave instructions about the trip. "You'll be leaving in the morning with
George Barry on our Cessna float plane. Be down at 8:30 A.M."

Next morning we took off as planned, but a faulty altimeter
brought us down again after one spin around Uranium City. "I'll
have to fix that," George said.

After an hour's delay we were again in the air. After an hour's
flying time out of Athabasca Lake, George yelled, "See the
change! From here on north it's. . .the Barrens."

It was a noticeable change, all right, but not too abrupt. The last
of the dwindling Hudsonian taiga forest does not surrender to the
Arctic without visible struggle. For a long time we were looking
down onto the transition zone—less and less greenery and more
and more lakes, and ever smaller and more stunted trees. Gradually
there came into view a patchwork of open brown prairie. In
another hour the change was distinct. Now we were viewing a
seemingly forgotten land marked more by tundra than forest, a vast
purplish region where the tide was definitely turning on the side of
the frozen north.

Our destination was Aberdeen Lake in the Thelon River country
in the central so-called Canadian Barrens. My mission was, of
course, that long-planned rendezvous with "Caribou Bob" Ruttan.

When three hours had gone by it was obvious that we had left
all trees behind. Now far and wide was an incredible awe-inspiring

Robert A. Ruttan, Canadian wildlife biologist, downs a caribou for the camp.

vista: rolling grassland, rocky ridges, and hundreds of mirrored, odd-shaped glacial lakes. Gone were the dwarfed evergreens, the stunted groves of birch and willow. Now was only tundra, rocks, and water. And for the first time we began noticing white cakes of ice on some lakes and here and there patches of snow. But it was the lakes that stood out. So numerous they were that a hundred could be counted at any one time. In some quick mental arithmetic I surmised that the Canadian Arctic must have at least a million lakes.

When our float plane finally settled onto Aberdeen Lake and glided ashore, a band of Eskimos, led by my host, "Caribou Bob," waded out to greet us. "Welcome to the Arctic," Bob said, "it's been a long correspondence and I'm glad you're here." This was the Thelon River caribou tagging camp where in four seasons Bob and his Eskimo team had tagged over five thousand wandering caribou, or as the Eskimos say, tuk-tu.

I had corresponded frequently with Bob in the late months while he was getting the operation ready and, now, at last, I was here. It was a good feeling. The camp consisted merely of several tents and three canoes with motors. But Bob soon told me the disappointing news: the migrating hordes of caribou had already passed Aberdeen. For three weeks his camp was the scene of busy tagging operations. The northward march of caribou had been on since the 25th of June, and the taggers had earmarked over fifteen hundred animals.

With the main herds gone, Bob's decision was to move operations three hundred miles to the northwest to Contwoyto Lake. This huge lake, eighty miles long by ten miles wide, lies directly in the path of another caribou herd. Bob had reasons to go there. He observed that the large westernmost herd (which he had named the Bathurst Inlet herd because of its summer range) could be intercepted on its southward migration and, if we were lucky, another large group could be tagged. In a few short hours, equipment was packed, wages were distributed, and with many handshakes we bid farewell. The sturdy, warm-hearted Eskimos and *Tuk-tu-Laree* (Bob's Eskimo name) had worked together four years and developed quite a friendship, so parting was not easy.

Soon we had all of Bob's equipment aboard, including a canoe strapped to the belly of the plane, plus a few reminders that we were in the summer Arctic. The first unavoidable and most noticeable confrontation one observes in the Barrens is its insects —mosquitoes, gnats, and fish flies. The last two are annoying and troublesome, but the mosquitoes are unbearable.

"We just stand them," Bob said. But for a full six weeks during July and August these tormentors, referred to generally as "flies," are so savage, so persistent that nothing escapes them. At times their blood-boring onslaught will drive some animals and humans mad. Repellants, such as 6-12 and Off, help some but only for a short period. Soon the attack is on again in full scale and the chosen victim made miserable. Head nets provide some relief for those who can stand them, and mosquito bars over sleeping bags at night are a salvation. But generally one must simply grit his teeth and take it.

We fogged the inside of the plane with repellant and took off, Bob sitting on a gas drum behind us. Our second stop three hours later was Pellatt Lake, a refueling base and game camp, where we met Bob's old friend and game officer, Jim McAuley, who arranged to employ a new band of Eskimos to help us. Jim prepared coffee and cooked a sumptuous meal of the fresh steaks I had brought with me from Uranium City. It was midnight as we ate, while the sun barely dipped over the horizon. We ate and talked and the talk was all caribou.

Pellatt Lake lies south of Contwoyto and is only a one-day canoe trip from the new tagging site. Bob was anxious to move north quickly but decided to go to Yellowknife next day for supplies. He and the pilot returned the following day and brought another game assistant and his wife with him. Two days later we were established on the east shore of Contwoyto and camped out on a hilly peninsula smack in the center of a caribou highway. Now all we had to do was find the caribou, await their coming, and catch them for tagging at the inlet crossings.

Besides Bob and myself, our final tagging camp crew consisted of Archie Mandeville, the game assistant from Yellowknife, his wife, and four good-natured Eskimos. Archie was a big hulk of a man, as strong as a musk-ox, northern born, bush raised, part Chipewyan, part French Canadian. He grew up with a Syrian trader, trapped and prospected over much of the north country, and spoke English, French, Cree, and Chipewyan. Our Eskimo crew was of the western ethnic group, which only recently came down from the coast around Bathurst. They spoke a different dialect from the Aberdeen Lake Eskimos.

Bob explained that the Eskimos had taken Christian first names although generally an Eskimo has only one name. Thus we had Simon (Kadlun), Joseph (Niptanatiuk), his son, James (Koonana), his nephew, and Amy (Mimilena), his daughter. The main families of our Eskimo crew remained back at Pellatt Lake where they were busy putting up fish and caribou meat for the winter. The men of

Jim McCauley, veteran game protector in the Canadian Arctic,
cleans Arctic lake trout for dinner.

our special crew helped with the boats and tagging, while Amy, an
attractive 21-year-old single girl, tended camp and doubled as
cook. All four spoke a little broken English, but Amy who spoke
best acted as chief interpreter. Our friends laughed a great deal,
usually replying to most queries with a simple gutteral "yuk."

The Canadian Arctic, it seems, harbors some five thousand Eskimos. More than half of these are maritime groups who dwell in and around the Arctic Archipelago and subsist largely on seal and walrus, coming inland only to hunt caribou. The others occupy the northern and central barrens and depend on caribou and Arctic lake trout for their diet. Often referred to as the Caribou Eskimos, they are docile, honest, friendly, and have a quiet determination to live out their special lives in a very special though hostile environment. The barrenland Eskimo is tied to the caribou much as the Pacific Aleut is tied to his salmon. Without caribou his life in the frozen Arctic, as he has known it for centuries, would be impossible.

Camels of the Frozen North

The caribou, upon which the Eskimos depend, have been called the *camels of the frozen north*. When domesticated, as in northern Europe, these large herd members of the deer family have come to be known as *reindeer*. Despite the prominence given them by Clement Moore's famed "A Visit from St. Nicholas," little of scien-

Caribou migration near Lake Contwoyto.

tific extent and depth had been known of the domestic and wild forms in Canada until the last decade. It was then that the Canadian Wildlife Service began its caribou investigations in earnest.

With the one exception of the musk-ox, caribou live farther north than any other hoofed mammal. They range in winter through much of the northern coniferous forests in both the New and Old World. However, in the wild state they are more common in the western hemisphere, notably Canada, with smaller populations in Alaska.

Caribou occur in three forms, possibly even a fourth. The woodland caribou roams the coniferous woodlands from Newfoundland and Labrador across to Alaska. It migrates only short distances, usually from the lower ranges to higher pastures and back again. In contrast the barren-ground caribou, which is only slightly smaller and more whitish than its woodland cousin, is a wide traveler. Some mammalogists believe that the allied forms of caribou, notably the Greenland caribou, mountain caribou, even the dwarf caribou of Queen Charlotte Island, are simply varieties of the barren-ground caribou *(Rangifer arcticus)*.

There is much misinformation about caribou in general, particularly about the haunts, habits, and numbers of the barren-ground species. Today scientific investigations are beginning to disclose the true nature of these wide-ranging animals, how they live, where they migrate, what they eat, and something of their population trends.

While it is true that barren-ground caribou migrate many hundreds of miles between their summer and winter ranges, some herds are known to migrate extraordinary distances, as much as a thousand miles in the spring and again in the fall. According to "Caribou Bob," the straight line migratory distance of his tagged animals from tag site to kill is about five hundred miles, or roughly one-third the annual migration distance.

What is probably not true is the estimate of their earlier numbers. These early-day guesses must be viewed with question. Scientific logic discredits the possibility of caribou numbers in earlier times going as high as twenty-five or thirty million animals. While the woodland caribou has dwindled in numbers and vanished from much of its former range and even totally disappeared from some areas, the barren-ground caribou, while apparently somewhat cyclic, has held its own and now seems on the increase.

Today there are probably more than four hundred to five hundred

Author with Bathurst inlet Eskimos.

thousand caribou on the Canadian Barrens, although a few biologists
would be surprised if the figure actually did go to a million. Even
in the best of times, then, it is seriously doubted if the Canadian
Barrens ever harbored more than one or two million caribou, and
then only for short periods. The available range and the known carrying capacity of summer and winter habitats simply preclude the
possibility of much higher populations.

For a full week after establishing our camp at Contwoyto we
scanned the skyline with binoculars, but no caribou showed up.
"You can easily miss them," said Archie one afternoon as we
trudged across the tundra. "You have to be on the constant look-
out." Then, one day in a chartered aircraft, Bob and I took off
northward for the Burnside and Hood rivers and the country around
the Arctic Sound. We reconnoitered the rugged seashore coast region around Bathurst Inlet, talked with a coast group of Eskimos,
but saw no caribou. There were compensations, however. We were
excited to see several herds of musk-oxen and one lone, defiant
bull musk-ox. But the caribou weren't revealing themselves.

"Somewhere in this vast country," Bob said, "there's a hundred thousand caribou, and we've got to find them." Caribou are not easy to spot. Their shaggy, white-brown coats blend into the rocky landscape, and even great herds can be mistaken for boulders and rocks.

Fascinating Country

The land of the tuk-tu is a fascinating place. There is much to see and do on slow days, especially for those willing to explore or help with supplying larder for the camp. Wildflowers bloom everywhere—Labrador tea, baked appleberry, Arctic sunflower, heather, and Arctic cottongrass. Many flower forms are tiny, like the dwarf cranberry, Arctic pink, and rhododendron. Some are so small as to be hardly seen with the naked eye. Others are microscopic. One of the most common of plants is the lichen. Though several species of lichen grow on the dry Barrens, they grow slowly, remain small, and hardly seem an important food item for the caribou.

Actually, the principal summer foods of the barren-ground caribou are not lichen but grasses, sedges, dwarf birch, and Arctic willow. However, when the caribou herds spread laterally through the tree country in the winter, their principal foods are the grey-white ground lichen, known to laymen as *reindeer or caribou moss*. Young calves are prone to eat more lichen, and this tendency, according to Bob, may be one of the attractions of the calving grounds in the summer.

Rainfall is low in the Barrens, averaging less than fourteen inches a year. But when the infrequent summer showers come, the prairies virtually come alive with plants, much as one finds in the desert. The grasses and low woody plants green up, the flowers explode in color almost overnight, and gray-brown mushrooms suddenly pop into view.

One day Archie and I picked a hatful of boleti. I knew them well, and when these were brought to camp and cooked and samples eaten, and no one seemed the worse for it, a sense of real achievement prevailed. From then on a great interest developed in mushrooms, and Camp Contwoyto was well supplied with edible fungi. Everyone agreed that a new and strange welcome was brought to our monotonous diet—canned meat and Arctic lake trout. Fresh lake trout are fine but one gets tired of even the best of fish.

Most of the deeper glacial lakes and the streams that flow from them are inhabited by Arctic lake trout, a true inland char that supplies much of the protein needed by the Eskimos. The fish gener-

Author and seaplane pilot prepare for Arctic char fishing.

ally run large, five to twenty and even thirty pounds, and piscatori-
ally prove as ravenous and rambunctious as any fish on tackle. The
food supply is scarce in the virgin waters so that most lakers are
forced to feed on lesser members of their own kind and on small
rocksnails and mosquitoes. The flesh of an Arctic laker is orange-
pink and when baked, boiled, or broiled, is as delicate and flavor-
some as any trout or salmon.

Bob Ruttan plays an Arctic lake trout.

Author landing a lake trout from Pellatt Lake, central Arctic.

Author admires lake trout.

Arctic lake trout in the water.

Two Arctic lake trout from Lake Contwoyto.

Author carries out two nice Arctic lake trout for the camp.

Author with prize lake trout.

Caribou at Last

On the ninth day at Contwoyto apprehension began rising at our tagging camp, and when our charter plane arrived from Yellowknife, Bob, Clem Baker the pilot, and I took off immediately on a recon trip toward Mara Lake, which Bob said was our "last hope."

As we neared Mara Lake, Bob shouted "Caribou!"

"Aw, go on," Clem shouted back. "I looked that rockpile over when we passed it. They're rocks!"

They were caribou alright—thousands of them. They stretched out for miles, a great mass of flowing animaldom over the Arctic landscape. My heart pounded in my ears. We circled and came down over them while I snapped pictures as waves of stampeding

Barren Ground caribou on tundra near Mara Lake, central Arctic.

Caribou migration near Mara Lake, south of Bathurst Inlet.

hooves burst across the tundra. We repeated our five-hundred foot maneuver several times, then selected a lake a few miles ahead in their path, and headed for a landing. The object was to quietly intercept them on foot, get more photos, and do some censusing.

The maneuver worked perfectly. We landed and took off across the country, heads low. The herd was coming in our direction alright but no animals showed yet on the skyline. But we could hear a massive rumbling in the distance, like thunder. My heart began to pound once more. Then the first of several bulls appeared on the skyline a quarter mile away. These lead animals carried enormous rocking-chairlike antlers, and when joined by others, gave the appearance of moving trees. More appeared and still more—bulls and cows and young. We hugged the ground, seeking the protection of large boulders, and presently in the shadows of two large rocks, we took up our stations. Bob and Clem began counting from one rock while I set up my camera in front of another.

Another view of migrating caribou near Mara Lake.

The caribou began forming a semicircle around us, and for the first time, we could hear the clicking of their feet, a characteristic snapping of the bone joints and of their big flexible hooves. And now out of the rumbling and thunder of their passage we began to detect the piglike *grunk-grunk* of the cows and the similar but higher pitched voices of the calves. Soon caribou were all around us, moving, snorting, clicking in an ever-increasing horde. Soon thousands of animals were crowded all around, a mass of moving wild animals such as few persons have seen. Thousands more headed straight for us—a hundred yards away, then fifty, then twenty, and then splitting as they detected us. We remained as motionless as marmots while still taking pictures, counting bulls, dry cows, cows with young, yearlings, and separate calves. My own heart pounded great drums in my chest as I thrilled to this great spectacle.

On they came in wave after wave, some passing as close as ten yards, others halting, growing suspicious after a long, hard look and suddenly bolting. Now and then an alert bull sensed something strange, halted, and dropped his head. Then not liking what he saw or smelled, stretched out his right rear leg to full length, and suddenly took off in a loping gallop, stampeding hundreds, thousands of other animals. The roar from such a maneuver was like some great Niagara turned loose.

For a full two hours the herd passed us. At times it seemed as if the whole tundra was a mass of caribou. Yet this was only the advance corps of the main Bathurst herd, which Bob estimated at around eighty-five thousand animals. As it turned out, an even larger herd was passing around the other side of Mara Lake at that very moment. "The total herd must number two hundred thousand," Bob said.

View of migrating caribou from a Cessna plane.

Part of the Bathurst Inlet caribou herd.

When the last of the herd finally passed us, the sun was falling fast and we had to get out of the country. Even though a breeze had picked up, Clem was worried and decided to take off alone and land again on a larger lake nearby. The scheme worked out well and after an hour we were in the air again.

At camp, it was soon all *tuk-tu amihut,* which means *many caribou* in Eskimo. Excitement mounted, and for four days thereafter it was all caribou talk: Were they heading our way? When would they reach us? Would they cross at the inlets expected? Was everything ready for the tagging?

A week later all questions were answered. The caribou came, although at points farther north than expected. Then a crowning blow fell. A freezing and fly-destroying northwest wind sprang up and blew constantly for several days. The entire herd, excepting a few relatively small groups, turned into it and moved steadily away

Caribou herds banding up.

Stampeding caribou.

Caribou on migration.

from the best tagging sites, to pass around the far end of Contwoyto Lake before swinging southward on their old route to
treeline. However, even then the alert and ever-watchful team of
Eskimo hunters were able to catch and tag in the water more than
three hundred animals.

The techniques used in this operation are simple enough, although not without danger to the taggers. The animals are caught
swimming in the water and each is brought to the gunwhale of the
tagging boat, a canoe, by using a long-handled shepherd's crook.
The animal is banded in the ear with a metal tag to which is attached a short, red flourescent vinyl streamer. The animal is then
released. Tagged animals can thus be seen more clearly and spotted
more easily from the air or when taken during the fall hunting season in the tree country far to the south where the caribou spread
out. By recovering tags from the animals, biologists can find out
how far the animals migrate and where they go, and can obtain
much other useful data so basic to good caribou management.

Several valuable facts are now beginning to come to light through these investigations. Tagging has revealed that at least three large and fairly distinct herds occupy the Arctic mainland between Hudson Bay (Baker Lake to Churchill) and the MacKenzie Valley. And although these herds do overlap and mix on their winter range, they "home" to their own summer ranges where they can be counted and thence managed according to the needs of the herd and the people of the area. Previous to tagging, investigators tended to underestimate actual numbers because of fear of duplication in counts where the herds were mixed.

The end result of these investigations is showing that present numbers are now reaching rather high levels. Investigations also tend to show that sound biological facts, and intelligent population management measures based upon such facts, plus the maintenance of the natural caribou habitat, are essential to keeping the barren-ground caribou healthy—and in a balanced relationship to essential

Massive caribou migration.

Two young Eskimos examine caribou trails on the Arctic tundra.

food supplies for the present and future populations. Anything short of this does not seem to be enough. And as Bob Ruttan related to me as I was leaving the Arctic Barrens, ''Surely the preservation of the last of these great herd animals of North America is well worth it.''

I agreed.

6
Incredible People

At Controyto I had my first opportunity to live with and learn something firsthand of the Eskimos. Our small work group was ideal for study. I found them quiet, friendly, and warmhearted, a small but strong and sturdy people with straight black hair and somewhat oriental faces and eyes. I asked quite a few questions because this was a way to engage them in conversation, and in the days that followed I discovered myself picking up a few native words, like *tuk-tu,* meaning caribou and *oomingmak,* the bearded one, referring, of course, to the musk-ox.

Up to this point my contact with Eskimos was only casual. I had seen them around Churchill and talked with a few at Point Barrow. Those around Yellowknife and Innuvik seemed a little shy and distant. Now I had the chance to know them intimately, and my summer with them on the Barrens promised to be a revealing experience.

Bob said I would return to the outside with an altogether different point of view of them, like he did when he first came into this country. It was obvious that he was thinking of a deeper respect for them, as the average white holds them to be somewhat primitive, unsanitary, and dull.

"They're not that way at all," Bob said. "In all my travels up here I've never found one to be unclean in habit or immodest. You'll never see one taking care of his personal needs, openly, like we often do."

In the days that followed I learned much from the Eskimos themselves and from Bob. I also brought along some reading material that was helpful.

The history of the Eskimo in North America is a fascinating story. Ethnologists, anthropologists, and archaeologists agree these people are a remarkable ethnic race. Some experts on Eskimo culture, with whom I have talked since, consider these people the most unique if not the most remarkable of aborigines in the New World. Apparently the belief is universal that these people came out of central Asia. The feeling is that they emigrated across some six thousand miles of the Arctic coastland from Cape Siberia and moved all the way to eastern Greenland. These people, furthermore, are surprisingly uniform in many ways—in physical characteristics, habits, and language. Nowhere else on the globe did an aborigine ethnic group spread itself so widely over so much northern land as did the Eskimo.

For some time many ethnologists believed that these people were latecomers to the New World. Now there is sufficient archaeological proof to show that this is not so. Recent discoveries show that the Eskimo was well established in his western sector at the time of Christ and even some years before. Remains of pottery, stone implements, and artifacts tested with carbon 14 show that these people were the real Eskimo ancients. They exhibited a very distinct culture a long time ago. There is belief too that even earlier remains of their existence may be found.

The Eskimo's origin in north central Asia is shrouded in archaeological obscurity. In Arctic Siberia the several languages and culture groups there are not like the more uniform culture of Arctic America. Their development resulted, apparently, from several separate movements northward. Some groups followed larger river courses to the Arctic coast. Artifacts from the Or River and Lake Baikal are said to resemble those of the ancient Eskimo. One of these great emigrations out of central Asia occurred around 200 to 50 B.C. It halted for a while at the Bering Sea, across from present-day Alaska, because of an unusual abundance of nature's riches—walrus, seal, and the beluga white whale. There were also fish and birds that gave the people a great sufficiency of everything, and they thrived.

As the population grew and the hardy men became proficient in their skin-covered oomiaks, they swarmed over the waters of the Straits, spilled over onto the Diomedes and other intermediate islands. Soon many of them established villages and small groups on the Alaskan coast. These were the Old Bering Sea People, small in stature but hardy, strong, and as courageous as any humans on earth. They stalked seals and huge bull walrus. Not infrequently, they attacked the king of Arctic beasts, the polar bear. When great black and white killer whales schooled in the ice waters, throngs of fearless men and courageous older boys took their oomiaks and put into the choppy waters and attacked the killers. The savage whales fought back tearing at the small boats, but the sharp harpoons finally proved too much and the waters turned red. Soon enormous white-black bellies floated to the surface. Then the work of recovering the carcasses of the huge beasts would begin.

Some of these ancient maritime dwellers paid for their feats with their lives—but the spirit that dwelled within them survived and strengthened. Ethnologists say that these Bering Sea People are the first Eskimos of which we have definite knowledge, yet there is general belief that a still earlier group came from coastal, northeastern Asia and spread into Arctic America.

One morning at Contwoyto, as our Eskimo friends squatted with us in the cook tent and the North Wind howled outside, the conversation turned to our gasoline stove. Amy was boiling—not brewing—coffee. Bob as usual was talking about caribou when suddenly the pressure in the stove gave out. As Amy went through the motions of pumping up the air tank and relighting the stove, I asked her how the early Eskimos made a fire.

She did not answer right away but faced her stove. Then she turned around and with a twinkle in her eyes and a smile, said "Matches."

"No, no," I corrected. "I mean in the early days, when they had no matches."

She said nothing. Brief silence before answering a question is characteristic of the Eskimos. Then she looked out and spoke something to Joseph. He in turn, smiled and giggled a little, and in turn mumbled something guttural to Simon. Now the old man had to answer. His eyes twinkled, he hissed a smile and drew in air between his teeth and drooping pipe. The pipe never seemed to leave his lips.

"Imbushook," or something like it, Simon answered. Amy hesitated and then said "by hitting two iron rocks."

Months later when I was in Washington, D.C., I checked on this and Simon was right. The aboriginal Eskimos made fire by taking two iron pyrites and striking them together to send sparks into tinder. The tinder could be most anything like musk-ox wool, dried Arctic cottongrass balls, or even human hair. The larger the rocks, the greater was the spark and the easier to get the fire started. Once a fire got going in a village or camp, it almost never was allowed to go out. Someone always would have a fire from which others could be ignited. Most fires were kept aflame in stone lamps into which was inserted a wick of dry moss. The lamps not only provided some heat for the snowhouses but also interior light during the long, dark winters. Rock fires provided the heat necessary for cooking. The vessels for cooking were mainly of the round and deep type and made of pottery.

From the Alaskan northwest the Bering Sea Eskimos pushed outward. One group moved along the coast northeastward, another southward. Then about a thousand years later a sudden expansion occurred, perhaps motivated by new tools and ideas coming over from Asia. New and better inventions of iron and shale and bone brought good times and the population soared. The resulting pressures moved the Eskimos still further eastward along the coast and did not stop until they reached Greenland and Baffinland. So bold, so swift was the eastern expansion that the Eskimos encountered no other inhabitants until they reached Hudson Bay.

Today archaeologists refer to the Bering Sea Eskimos as Panuk and those in the Eastern Arctic as Thule. Customs have changed considerably and there now is some seasonal migration, especially among those populations of the Central Arctic. In the winter the Eskimos stayed close to the sea ice, living off seal and walrus. During the summer they moved inland in search of caribou, musk-ox, small mammals, birds, and fish.

In comparatively recent times some of the so-called caribou Eskimos stayed on in the Arctic barrens all year long, moving only slightly from one hunting and trapping territory to the next. To ease their take of caribou in Canada the government began to subsidize certain groups with food, clothing, and other provisions. They set up schools for them such as the one at Innuvik, 350 miles north of the Arctic Circle, in the MacKenzie Delta.

I asked Amy one day how she liked her three years in school at civilized Innuvik and she replied hesitatingly with a high-pitched "I like it." But the truth is modern life in most northern villages offers little but degradation to the freedom-loving, self-reliant Eskimo. Perhaps Simon put it most clearly when he said that Indian

Author (right) with Bathurst Inlet Eskimos.

A trapper's cache at the Arctic Circle, Alaska.

and white man villages "no good. . .just shovel white man's garbage and ——."

In the true Arctic the Eskimo is still loose, still untied like the
North Wind. His wants are few, pleasures simple. His load is arduous but not unpleasant. With traded furs and skins he can now
buy tobacco and groceries and such rare luxuries as boats, motors,
gasoline, even Skidoos. Yet much of the Eskimo's life even today
is primitive, living in tents or shacks in the summer and snowhouses in the winter, traveling along inland and coastal waters in
the summer by kayak and the roomier umiak, a large boat used
mainly to transport family groups. In the winter travel is on foot,
dog team, or Skidoo.

Like the Indian tribes in and around the tree country, the Crees
and Chipeweyans, the Eskimos keep lots of dogs, but unlike their
traditional enemies, they treat their canines well. Indians often

starve their dogs in the summer, taking back the stragglers and the most hardy when cold weather arrives and their usefulness is once more apparent. Not so the Eskimo. His dogs are well cared for all year through.

I asked Joseph why this was so and he grinned. Simon smiled. Amy said nothing. They knew the answer but would not say.

"It's because the Indian has become contaminated with the ugly ways of the white man," Bob put in. Amy blushed a little and turned to her teapot on the stove. There was a moment of silence. Then she turned around, grinned, and announced, "Tea ready."

7
Mystique and Myths

Slowly, almost imperceptibly, the great black mantle of darkness began to fade. At first there was merely a suggestion of grayness, like the shade of charcoal gray cloth that is hard to distinguish from black, then gradually the sky lightened and I was impelled to view the change fully. I threw back the mosquito netting and raised my head out of the sleeping bag. Dawn was definitely breaking over the slumbering Arctic.

The night had been brief. One's body accustomed to eight hours of sleep is quick to reveal it. One would like to rest more but the urge to be awake and about in this haunting land is persistent and strong. Even in the middle of the night in a kind of semiconsciousness one is aware of a strange power in this land, one that is at once inviting and at times, repelling, yet always strongest on the side of the former. Now the sky was beginning to yield to an ashy whiteness and wisps of pink plumed light began to show up. The promise was too much for lying in a bag and I broke out of it and arose, stretching in the morn's vigorous chill. But to see the full glory of an Arctic morn one should see it from a hill.

Near at hand was a small esker. It was a hillock of glacial gravel uneven and rough, and definitely not for sleeping. It lay too exposed and received the full blast of cold winds from across the frozen ice. But for observation, for viewing the vast landscape of land and water, the ice and sky, no place came better.

The climb to the esker's summit was enough to make my blood circulate freely. I sat down on a small round rock and momentarily closed my eyes. A breeze was picking up and it rustled over the exposed patches of sand on the hill, making an ever so gentle sifting sound. In a few moments the entire landscape unfurled itself on every side in a faint whiteness and rays of orange began to streak across the eastern sky. Now all was light once more. The pageant of a vast, remorseless land had undraped itself again on an enormous stage. I kept closing and opening my eyes and listening.

There is a profound silence in the Arctic. It is a pervasive, all encompassing kind of a silence and it digs deeply into your bones. Every mosquito, it seems, every sand grain rolling over, every lap of water against the melting ice, is picked up by the inner ear, and some of these from great distances. The carrier of these sound waves, even the faintest of them, is the moving breeze. The deepest silence, the very epitome of all quiet, comes when all air seemingly stops moving. Then the silence is astounding. Such a silence is nowhere else to be experienced, except perhaps in a cave. When a sharp sound breaks the spell, it carries incredibly long distances. True Arctic stillness suggests a remoteness, a type of aloneness, that defies description.

As I watched the Arctic morning unfold I began to wonder about what it is that draws a man to the far north country, to venture out on to desolate barrens and to sleep on the ground and to climb an esker to see a strange world come to life.

Now the view was one of a breathtaking panorama. All became purple and yellow and gold. Only the ice, etched as sheets of ivory across the lake, and the dull green of melted water, stood out in contrast. The purple was land, rocks, and exposed sweeps of gravel and limestone, and an endless patchwork of grasses, sedge, and dwarf birch. No trees silhouetted the skyline, no man-made objects disturbed the wildness of this land where the raw elements of the planet never seemed tamed.

Yes, why does one come to such a place? Surely there are good reasons. First, and perhaps most plausibly, I would have to say that one comes to such a place because it is here; it is the Arctic. Just as Mt. Everest is there, so too the Arctic is here to explore. And so long as we have this special world—and so long as we have an Everest, a Kilamanjaro—men, I suspect, will seek them out.

There seems yet a more rational reason for a sojourn in the Arctic. What about the myths of this land? What about the legends?

An esker hillock in the central Canadian Barrens.

Could another reason for coming be to investigate its myths and legends, to discover its reality and separate truth from fiction?

The search for truth by man is an irrepressible search, and I felt satisfied for the moment that my coming to the esker had reasons beyond simply the joys of travel. As a wildlife biologist I felt I wanted to see and experience firsthand for myself something of the wonder as well as the fearsome qualities of the Far North.

While there is much that is known about the Arctic tundra today, much more yet remains to be discovered. Some things suggest only partial truth and many aspects only myth. The stories about lemmings and lichens are cases in point.

Many people think of lemmings, for example, as birds because this is what the name sounds like. But lemmings are really mouselike rodents, creatures of the north that periodically develop into prodigious numbers. Lemmings, we have been told, multiply into enormous hordes that move across the tundra by the millions—moving like some grasshopper plague over the timeless Arctic plains, running, scurrying, moving endlessly, and not stopping until they reach the sea, there only to hurl themselves into the frigid waters in a mass suicidal death.

This is the mythology of the lemmings. Yet there is a reality to these rodents in the Arctic and the stories that the lemmings come down from the mountains to commit certain self-destruction is not without some truth. These creatures indeed do come out of the hills of Norway by the thousands, like a locus plague; they do sweep everything before them, moving constantly onward toward the fjords and bays and, there, sometimes plunging to certain death in the sea. Yet much of the picture in the Old World and even more so in the New World is fictional.

Lemmings do build up in numbers, they do move, but the reality of their travels and the exact physiological forces that trigger these reactions remain very much of a mystery.

How the stories of lemmings marching *en masse* to the sea to commit certain suicide ever got started, no one really knows. Some observers who saw this happen on a minor scale might have magnified the story all out of proportion to the truth, and then the stories grew. Studies today show that lemmings do not really travel great distances, even when their cyclic numbers are high. Thus only a small portion of the total population is ever found around the Arctic coast. Secondly, the drownings that occur are the result of attempts to cross areas of water in the path of their movement—streams, ponds, lakes, bays, and other bodies of water. Some individuals make it, others do not. If the crossing is formidable, then all who attempt it perish. Moreover, the so-called migration is not a long-distance trek at all. It is mostly an instinctive attempt to go from a range of limited food supply to one of more abundance.

Just what happens to the lemmings is not easy to explain because no one really knows the answer. One plausible explanation, not without some scientific basis, is that when lemming populations build up, a natural mechanism comes into play which causes the hungriest and weakest of the rodents to be nervous. Soon, these individuals gain an impulse to move, to get out, and soon one by one these restless ones begin to travel. Soon a whole emigration is on in full swing. The healthiest of the lemmings apparently remain behind and when their ranks are appreciably depleted the natural balance of food and rodents is again restored. Meanwhile, the emigrating group moves outward until a new food supply is found, when the animals once again revert to their normal behavior. If when in the process of emigrating outward they meet certain barriers, like a pond or sea, they attempt to cross it and in doing so perish. But mass suicide is obviously not one of nature's ways of balancing lemming populations with food supply. Certainly I saw no evidence of this in my Arctic travels in the New World.

North American lemmings are rather easily distinguished from mice but are confused with the lesser known voles and phenacomys. Most mice have large ears and long tails and a more pronounced head. Lemmings have very short ears and tail and a head that is small and almost indistinguishable from the rest of the body—giving these animals the appearance of small brown balls of fur.

Lemmings are among the most brilliantly colored of the Arctic rodents. One species, the collared lemming, is the only small, mouselike mammal that turns white in the winter. Voles are very much like the lemmings except for a longer tail and slightly larger ears. The phenacomys are volelike rodents, also with tails longer than those of the lemmings, but are more distinctly common in the cold forest regions of Canada and the high mountains of western United States. All voles have a tail longer than one inch. But all rodents of this type whose tails measure less than one inch are lemmings.

The species of lemming encountered most in the North American tundra is the Greenland collared lemming. Several others occur in lesser numbers on the tundra, notably the Hudson Bay lemming, found east of Hudson Bay, and the Unalaska collared lemming, known only from Unalaska and Umnal Islands, Alaska. The common brown lemming also occurs in the tundra but has a range into the tree country of southwestern Canada and across Alaska. Lemmings, I have found, are not too common in the New World and sizeable emigrations seem to be rare. In all my sojourns in the North I have seen only a half dozen of these small inhabitants of the Far North.

As the sun rose over the silent land I kept training my binoculars on likely looking places for lemmings but never saw a single one. Not satisfied, I decided to make a whole day's search of it—to make a thoroughly expert search for lemmings. I walked and searched, listened, glassed rock piles, lodges, tundra flats. I checked all possible hiding places where lemmings might live, and, by nightfall, had canvassed a ten-square-mile area. My full count of lemmings in a fourteen-hour search totalled exactly zero.

The next day I was out again on the tundra but this time I decided to investigate another form of life—lichen.

What about the lichen? What are these strange looking plants and just what is supposed to be their relationship to such animals as the caribou? Do caribou really subsist largely on lichen, these supposedly plush, lettucelike plants of the tundra?

Or, was this just another myth that needed exploring?

My travels in the Arctic soon showed me that few lichens were lettucelike and watery in appearance. Few species, too, seemed large enough or succulent enough for herbivores to single out and eat. Most of the plants I had seen were tiny, dry, extremely slow-growing, and apparently without much food value.

Specifically, the lichen is a rudimentary plant. Until about two hundred years ago, most botanists lumped lichen in with the mosses, with whom they were associated. But about the middle of the last century it was discovered that lichen were not mosses at all but distinct separate plants. They were found to consist of a distinct but separate elementary fungus living in close association with a green algal plant. The bulk of the lichen body seemed to be a fungus, and buried within its form were algal cells. The two plants, one incapable of making its own food and the other capable of photosynthesis, together form the *thallus* of the lichen. This is the portion of the lichen one sees on rocks or growing around mosses and similar plants.

In my Arctic travels I have seen many species of lichen. Today botanists have identified hundreds of lichen in the world. More are being identified each year.

These plants are curiously related to the green stains found on tree trunks, including the tiny green or blue-green molds of lake waters, and of fungi related to the molds. The complex interrelationship of the fungal-algal body involves exchanges of chemicals as well as the more traditionally known manufacture of food by the green member of the pair, the alga, and the absorption of water by the enveloping fungus.

The *thallus* of the lichens takes many forms, including *crustose,* granular or angularly divided thin layers on rocks or tree trunks, *foliose* or leafy platelike or lobed bodies, and also *fruiticose* or shrubby forms that can take the form of unbranched spikes or cups, or knobbed clubs, or branched and intertangled stalks called *podetia.* Since these plant forms are partnerships, reproduction is quite unique. The principal method of reproduction is either by means of fragments breaking off the original plants or by the formation of powdery granules called *soredia* which contain cells of both members of the partnership. Small, corallike branchlets called *isidia* may also be formed and break off to reproduce the partnership.

In most plants the fungus produces spores in saclike *asci* in a layer in the saucer-shaped *apothecia*. However, these spores have to alight next to the proper alga under just the correct conditions for growth to form a new lichen, so that this is probably a less common means of reproduction.

Lichen have long been used as a source of dyes; Harris tweeds and litmus paper are familiar examples of the products of such dyestuffs. Some are used for food for humans in emergencies, others are more poisonous and, in fact, have been used in wolf poisons. A few are very important in the perfume trade, being used to make the many ingredients in perfumes. Some are used in the manufacture of antibiotics. Lichen also are important in the weathering and breakdown on rocks to form soil through the chemical action of lichen acid. On some soils lichen help to prevent wind or water erosion.

On the dry Arctic Barrens where I have traveled the lichen are small and slow-growing and seem only a minor part of the food intake of the summer-feeding Barren Ground caribou. If caribou had to live on these plants solely in the Arctic I'd dare say that there would be few such animals around today. It is only in wet boreal forests in the sub-Arctic Hudsonian wilderness where the caribou moss or *Cladonia* is eaten to any extent by caribou. But even here it is the woody shoots of trees and shrubs that make up the bulk of the caribou's diet.

There are many other misconceptions about the Arctic, such as its unremitting cold, the strangeness of the Eskimos, the absolute barrenness of the land, which need to be examined and corrected. I believe one way to do this is for observers to make more careful observations and then to better interpret the storylines in nature. What one sees in the natural world is not nearly as important as correct judgment and interpretation of what one sees.

Perhaps one of the most common misconceptions about the Arctic Barrens is the weather and the cold and the fact that man cannot survive in this seemingly terrible and hostile world. As has been pointed out the Barrens can be bleak and inhospitable and men have died in its vast desolate landscape. On the other hand men have survived in it, even under pretty rough conditions.

In early spring of 1967, on April 3 to be exact, a veteran bush pilot named Robert Gauchie had a hospital reunion with his wife and three daughters two months to that day since his plane disappeared in the bleak Barrens. He had survived fifty-nine days —alone, besieged by wolves, and with little but raw fish to eat—in temperatures that dropped to forty-eight degrees below zero.

Gauchie, 39, of Fort Smith, was being treated in Yellowknife District Hospital, N.W.T. for "general weakness and probably frostbite in both feet" following his rescue.

"I never gave up hope. If you give up hope, you're as good as gone in this country," Gauchie told his rescuer, Ronald Sheardown of Toronto.

Sheardown said that when he landed his plane on Lake Samandre, where Gauchie had put down February 2 after running out of fuel during a blizzard, Gauchie was able to walk to his rescuers.

"We shook hands, and then he smiled through a massive bushy beard," Sheardown said. "All he said was, I'm sure glad to see you guys."

Gauchie's fifty-nine-day endurance in the wastelands of the Arctic, beyond the northernmost treeline of the continent, rivaled the achievement of two Americans, Helen Klaben and Ralph Flores, who survived forty-eight days in the Yukon in 1963 after a plane crash.

Gauchie was spotted by Sheardown and Glenn Stevens. They said that Gauchie followed classic procedure and stayed by his plane. He told his rescuers a wolf pack maintained a constant vigil over his plane for the last couple weeks. He said he kept his rifle close at all times.

Sheardown said Gauchie told him he slept in his sleeping bag inside the aircraft and subsisted on a diet of fish and rations in a survival kit. He lost some fifty pounds during the two months. He occupied himself by keeping a day-by-day log.

"His mental and physical condition appeared excellent. He talked a lot on the flight and even joked about his ordeal," Sheardown said.

So the Arctic tundra can be withstood by man if he keeps his wits about him and keeps from doing foolish things.

8
Scourge of the Arctic

Every natural environment in America has its good and bad aspects. Eastern woods have their charm, their beauty but also poison ivy and thorn thickets. The seashore has its pleasant sounds, its balmy days but it has storms and gales that menace wildlife and man. The swamps, the grasslands, the marshes, and the mountain strongholds all have their wondrous nature. But they have their drawbacks too. So does the Arctic. The Arctic has beauty, bounty, but also a scourge. This is insects. Perhaps in no other place in the world are insects so numerous, so unbearable. I have made mention of this fact in a casual manner several times but because the situation with insects is so severe, I feel that this aspect of the Arctic deserves special mention.

For six to eight weeks in the summer, mostly in July and August, the insect menace, collectively referred to as *flies,* is so fierce that life for beast and man is made wretched.

Although the fish flies are members of the tiny gnat family and are pesky and the deer flies and blow flies are quite troublesome, the chief culprit of the "fly" scourge is the black Arctic mosquito—perhaps as vicious a speck of insect vengeance as ever came upon the earth. It persists in the low, wet areas of the tundra where the growth is low and thick, and the hiding places are ideal.

The tundra biome has three characteristic plant forms, the Arctic

107

grasses, the tundra sedge, and the dwarf birch. The first two seldom reach over a foot in height and the birches rarely get over eighteen inches above ground. These main plants dominate the tundra so insurgently that other lesser plants seem only to have filled in the gaps, like weeds in a vegetable or flower garden. Over much of the tundra the dwarf birch and, to a lesser degree, the Arctic willow spread over most tracts where they can take root, save the rutted trails of the caribou and rocky outcrop areas. In some places the birch forms spotty clumps with grass and sedge in bordering circles; in other spots it covers large areas not unlike low bush blueberry in New England. But unlike blueberry patches, the dwarf birch of the Arctic presents a shorn look, as if some mystic gardener had come along with a giant pair of shears and clipped it down to a foot-high level.

It is here and in the wet bogs of grasses and sedges where the mosquito finds ideal habitat. Here it persists and thrives. It is from these places that it launches its most savage onslaughts.

As soon as the sun thaws the snow patches and the lowlands begin to show blankets of green in June, the life of the mosquito, quiet for nine long months but not extinguished, begins to stir. After a few warming days the larvae escape from their tiny egg cases, wriggling, and in a few added days become pupae. Then the pupae emerge as winged insects and soon generation after generation of mosquitoes follow in rapid order. At first the insects stay among the wet and dark bushes and among the blades of grass, but as their numbers explode, they move outward, first laterally in great swarms, then upwards in great clouds of black madness. Soon their numbers are so great that solid blankets of them hover over the birches and low places and woe to the creature who passes near.

The heyday of the fly season lasts from the beginning of the summer solstice to about the middle of August. During this period the mosquitoes are everywhere—on high ground, in low areas, on the hills and eskers and mountains, in the valleys, among the dwarf willows and birches, among the heather and saxifrage, on all hummocks, all banks of streams, all lakes. Every twig, every blade of grass, every surface of every living thing sends thousands, millions of them into the air all day long. So thick and noisy are the mosquitoes at this point that they pelt one's face as does mist from a powerful spray and the sound from millions of vibrating wings is a continuous hum. In tropical countries the mosquito swarms by day but quiets down at night. Not so with the tundra tormentor. For six to eight weeks this merciless, small, black, bloodthirsty savage besieges the northland without let-up—hour after hour, all day and all night.

When a caribou or man walks into their domain, it is like walking barefaced into a beehive. The attackers form swarms around the invader until the victim seems as if enveloped in smoke. They shroud as with a fog every living creature that disrupts their home or passes by, only to follow as black smoke, attacking every inch, every millimeter of exposed flesh, and everywhere driving in tiny, fierce beaks and swelling their abdomens full with hot red blood. So dense do the swarms become at times that the victim can scarcely see or breathe. The only recourse is flight.

Ernest Thompson Seton in his *Arctic Prairies* tells of a count of mosquitoes he made on his exposed arm one day just to prove how unbelievable this scourge can be on the Arctic barrens in the summer: "In one five minute period I counted 254 of these black specks on my hand until I could stand it no longer. Then I smeared them away with my other hand, killing them in a mass of wet blood."

The only time that I've noticed any let-up in the mosquitoes was when the temperature dropped into the middle thirties and a strong wind would come up which made flying difficult. Even out on the open lakes, miles from shore, the mosquitoes followed us and kept up their relentless attack.

Migrating caribou are especially tormented by the summer scourge, a pitiful thing to see when the fly attack is on in full force. Some animals stop, drop their heads, then shake their muzzles in the grass, as if to try to wipe their noses and eyes; their skins switch, backs and bellies roll, feet kick and strike as they try desperately to ward off the attackers. Sometimes the onslaught is so unbearable that whole herds will begin to run, finally breaking into a stampede, heading for higher ground in search of a breeze or stronger wind. At other times the attack is so maddening that whole masses of caribou will head for water, and upon reaching it, go barrelling in like throngs of human bathers trying to escape the heat.

Fortunately for man, there is a measure of protection available. Repellants help, but only for short periods. Head nets, gloves, and mosquito bars are the best protection. The former has its disadvantages, being annoying and troublesome, and always interfering with visibility and eating. Yet it certainly is better than being eaten alive. At night a mosquito bar over one's sleeping bag provides welcome relief.

But even the mosquito in the Arctic, one supposes, has its place. Its larvae are fed upon extensively by fish, and adult mosquitoes, swarming over water and land, are eaten by small birds. So one must give the mosquito its place and try not to be unsympathetic to the important ecological role it surely plays in the great power cycle of life in the difficult North.

9
Magical World of the Tundra

The casual visitor to the Barrens may quickly conclude that this is a terribly dull place, and indeed this may have some partial truth if one flies in, quickly looks about, and departs. But this is no way to see any kind of land. Long ago in my travels I concluded that if one really wishes to see a country, to know it as it is, he must spend some time in it or, better yet, live in it.

I was beginning to get into this kind of questioning frame of mind after a few days on the Barrens when one afternoon a certain charge of expectancy began to develop around our camp. This feeling is difficult to explain. Perhaps it is due to a change in the weather, air pressure, or something else. Whatever the cause, one senses that an imminent change is about to occur and begins to prepare for it. It was very much like the day in the James Bay country when I heard the timber wolves. Now I felt a new mood coming to the Arctic.

I retired to our tent, crawled into my sleeping bag, and was soon off in drowseland. During the night—not a night really but a perpetual golden glow—I was awakened by the patter of rain against the tent, our first rain. It was a good sound, friendly, and its familiarity lulled me to sleep so deep and refreshing, so utterly delightful, and so completely relaxing, that my tent companions and I all snored heavily.

Author fishing for Arctic lake trout, Hood River, Arctic Barrens.

Start of the Arctic tundra near Hudson Bay, Manitoba.

The day before, Archie and I had taken one of those long tramps across the tundra and when bedtime came we felt dog-tired.

But the rain must have stopped long before dawn, and when we awoke, strong rays from the sun were already warming the tent. Caribou Bob crawled out from his rawhide sleeping bag naked as usual and announced it was going to be a good day. Archie grunted something agreeable down deep in his bag, then threw back the head flap, bursting "What a night. Haven't slept like this since last summer."

We dressed and one by one crawled and fanned our way out of the tent. "Great day alive," I exclaimed, "look at the wildflowers!" All around us, near and far, the tundra sparked and glowed with white, pink, yellow, and gold, a scene so breathtaking and heart-warming that I couldn't believe my eyes. Why only yesterday the barrens were brown, dry, and seemingly lifeless. True, there were few bunches of Labrador tea *(Ledum groenlandicum)* here and there, mostly in withered form, but nothing even faintly suggesting that this might happen.

"It's the rain," Bob said. "This is dry prairie country and rain does something to it—like the desert."

Amy popped her head out of the cook tent and announced that hot coffee was ready. But the spell of blooming wildflowers was too much for me and I couldn't resist a quick romp around the tent area for a few moments of looking and stimulating relaxation. A gentle breeze filtered in from the north bearing the sweet fragrance of bog rosemary *(Andromeda polifolia),* its tiny flowers appearing everywhere. Most abundant of all flowering forms seemed to be the whitish clusters of Labrador tea and the delicate, single straw-berrylike flowers simply referred to as bake apple. The latter is a common low berry plant in nearly all parts of Arctic and sub-Arctic Canada. In late August and early September it bears a small pumpkin-shaped fruit, the size of a man's thumbnail, and is colored whitish-pink and makes a mildly sweet and distinctively flavored preserve.

Throughout breakfast, consisting of porridge, bread and jam, and eggs, all washed down joyously with lots of Eskimo-style boiled coffee, we talked about the wildflowers. I had read about the sudden bloom of Arctic flowers, and saw lots of them around Hudson Bay, but this was different. One night of rain made the fantastic change.

"Why don't you just make a day of it?" Bob suggested. "You'll probably never get a better chance for pictures."

The point hardly had to be made. I was already planning just such a day in my mind and Bob's point propelled me through my meal all the faster.

In a half-hour I was well on the tundra heading for an unusually colorful mound covered with a mass of white plants. It was a hillock Archie pointed out to me, saying it had the best variety of Arctic flowers in the area. He said I couldn't miss it because it had three Eskimo graves on it and harbored a family of marmots; he referred to them as *sik-sik*.

The mound was beautiful. So awe-inspiring was the view from it and the flowering plantlife surrounding it that I just sat down on a boulder and remained there transfixed for a long time, as if in some far-off Garden of Gethsemene. True, it was a treeless wilderness garden but the sights and the mixed fragrance amid all the vast stillness was enough to send a fluttering, exhilerating chill down my spine. All around my feet were miniature forms of a floral world—the drooping pinks of a dwarf rhododendron *(Rhododendron lappanicium),* tiny aprons of delicate, starlike saxifrage *(Saxifraga tricuspidata),* garlands of buttercups smaller than a match head, miniature stems of grass-of-Parnassus, and many other rose and light purple flowers I could not identify.

I slipped off the boulder and dropped face down onto a cushion of embroidered magic. If only I had a camera that could pick up the beauty of this Lilliputian floral community, what a colorful story this would make. Here, not six inches before my eyes, was a patchwork of miniscule floral wreaths bound in soft blue and crimson, yellow and purple, white and gold, and from them my nostrils picked up a fragrance as delicate as the softest perfume.

Down off the hillside in the wetter areas between the higher points of land, the saxifrage grew in profusion on small mounds and clumps, surrounded by white festooned Arctic cottongrass and lush other grasses and sedges. The tussocks are small islands of climax vegetation in muskeglike country, only there are no trees. The only plants suggesting tree growth are the foot-high dwarf birch *(Betula sp.)* and the prostrate Arctic willow *(Salix sp.).* The willow is a remarkable plant in these environs and its flowering catkins, large for such dwarfed plants, seem incongruous to the human eye. They form a paradise for humming bees and fluttering butterflies.

The rain had turned the inch-long spikelets, according to the hues of stamen and pistil present, into shades of yellow, gold, pink, crimson, and even dark brown. For in the custom of all members of the great willow family, the sexes are on separate plants rather than being combined in one flower.

It is improper to refer to these lowlands where the dwarf willows grow as swamps or muskegs. Swamps are essentially wet places in the deciduous forest in the temperate zone, where the dominant vegetation is hardwood trees. In the Deep South, swamps are characterized by a mixture of red maple and gum trees; in more northern climes, by red maple, alder, and black willow. The important thing is that the term swamp should only be referred to low wet places that have forest growth.

Similarly, muskegs are wet places that are found in coniferous forest regions. They are normally open areas with pockets of water and soggy ground and surrounded by evergreen growth, usually black spruce. True muskegs are not found on the Arctic prairies but in the wetter coniferous Hudsonian forest region further to the south.

The dwarf willow in the tundra lowlands drapes itself over rocks and tussocks, spreading laterally to take advantage of the warmer temperatures. Some willows may spread themselves several feet giving a strange looking starlike pattern to their growth. These willows nevertheless are true trees and put on annual growth each year, although the yearly increment is very slow. One small willow stem that I cut away and later checked out for annual rings contained eighty-seven circles in an inch of growth. Some willows have been recorded with four hundred annual rings in a stem only one inch in diameter.

On my way back to camp I paused frequently to admire the brilliant but stunted Arctic sunflower, a ten-inch tall beauty of such golden radiance that no artist could truly capture its glow or its freshness. These were not plentiful—unusually the showy flowers seldom are—but those that displayed themselves here and there performed a service of great art. They looked like gems of sparkling gold in the midst of a floral carpet already amazingly beautiful.

Like flowers in the desert, the floral plants of the tundra are uniquely equipped for life in a hostile climate. For 270 to 300 days of the year the Arctic landscape, its lands and waters, remain immobilized by snow and ice. The soil is sour, poorly drained, cold, and a perpetual permafrost is found not far below the surface. Under such conditions the roots cannot go deep but must spread sideways. Thus the plants of the tundra are small and compact, with fibrous, spreading root systems and tough leaves and stalks. Many plant forms do not depend on seeds, but perpetuate themselves through root growth and by budding.

I stayed down in the tundra lowlands a long time, viewing from a tussock of cottongrass the natural beauty of this primeval world. I picked up a sedge plant and began examining its tassel of seeds. They were tiny and I had to reach for my hand lens to see the seeds. Now, two inches from my eye, was the phenomenon of remarkable life encased in a minute world, in seed after seed. Then I remembered what I had heard of the great longevity of Arctic seeds, how some were found to be viable after very long periods of time. Seeds of the Arctic tundra lupine, for example, which had lain frozen in tundra soil for ten thousand years, were germinated and found to produce normal healthy plants.

The hard-coated lupine seeds were found in lemming burrows some three to six yards deep in frozen silt near Miller Creek in the Yukon Territory, as reported by A. E. Porsild and C. R. Harington of the National Museum of Canada, and G. A. Mulligan of the Plant Research Institute, Canada. Remains of nesting material, skulls, skeletons, and other evidences of the lemmings were found.

The scientists believe some catastrophic event such as a landslide or precipitating volcanic ash buried the burrows in spring or early summer thousands of years ago, smothering the rodents and preventing the soil around from thawing, so the seeds remained dry and continually frozen.

The previous record for seed longevity may have been that of a sacred lotus, *Nelumbium nuciferum,* an old seed that sprouted after it had remained dormant in a far-Eastern peat bog for two thousand years.

On my way back I stopped several more times to admire various plants. On some stones the rock-clinging orange lichen caught my eye. This plant seems to flourish on rocky outcrops frequented by hawks and owls. The nitrogen-rich droppings left by the birds attract lichen and help them spread. Other lichen displayed every shade in the coloring book—delicate greens, soft yellows, deep purple, blue, white, red, and jet black.

In every land that belongs completely to nature there are compensations. The floral magical carpet of the summer tundra is one such compensation in a world that is largely cold and desolate. Were it not for the wildflowers, for the mosses and lichen, for the vestigial prostrate tree forms, the tundra of the Arctic would be much harder to take.

10
The Not So Loony Loon

Of all the birds in the Far North that typify the wildness of Arctic lands none is more fascinating than the loon. I have heard the loon sound its weird call in many places, in the northern Adirondacks, Maine, Michigan, Ontario, yet nowhere is one so moved by its call as on the tundra Barrens. Though the voice of the common loon—an easterly species—is weird enough, the sound of the red-throated loon on the desolate Arctic prairies is much more unnerving.

The red-throat gives out his call nearly always toward evening. At such times this alert and handsome bird appears to herald the coming of the long midnight glow. This loon calls most often during that period of the evening when a brisk wind springs up and starts to dissipate the warm air and the mosquitoes of the day.

For several evenings between the hours of eight and eleven the loons serenaded our camp on the quiet Barrens. Their song is a song of solitude punctuated by notes of hysterical melancholy. The ones we heard were obviously loners as their calls came separately from different corners of Lake Controyto. The cry of one loon in particular intrigued me. One evening I took a compass and time reading on him intent on paying him a visit some time. His call was peculiar at its end and markedly distinctive. Again and again he sounded his high-pitched laughter, the first notes always suggesting the shrieks of a strangling, dying woman. When this kept up for the longest time, my mind was made up. I was determined more than ever to find this creature the next evening and study his actions.

The common loon of more southern lands gives the appearance of a small goose, except for its pointed bill. It has a measure of difficulty getting off the water. This is not quite so with his cousin, the red-throat. Often on Contwoyto we would race over their placid cove in our canoe, only to see one startled and burst into the air, much as a mallard or black duck does in a small pond. This ability of the red-throat to readily break into the air without a splashing take-off seems to be the main difference between the two loons.

The next day, a half-hour before the appointed hour of the heralding loon, I put on my sweater, gloves, and head net and took off across the Barrens. The compass bearing led me to a small esker about a mile from camp where the Eskimos had a small burial ground. The evening was quiet. No wind stirred. It was a good time for listening and studying the mood of the summer Arctic. But no sooner had I reached the rocky promontory when a red-throat sounded his chilling call. It came from a small lagoon not far away. He was quite close for a loon but I wanted to ease into a better viewing position. Quietly and slowly I gained the top of the hill. Loons are like wild Canada geese, they like lots of distance between themselves and other moving things, especially humans. I knew this and was careful.

With the skill of a hunting Eskimo I finally gained the vantage point and there froze into position, eyes peeling the lake below, ears straining for every sound. But all my eyes and ears could pick up for the moment were mosquitoes. They milled around me by the thousands, like small black jets, and seemed to be growing madder every minute for not being able to get at me. I lifted back my head net, smeared on some repellent and took a hard look through the binoculars, but saw no loon. Suddenly, directly ahead of me on the still-fresh earth of an Eskimo grave, a sik-sik popped into view. The marmot was startled at seeing me and yanked his head down into a hole as if pulled down by a spring. Then, wanting another look, he was up again. We eyed each other at thirty feet for several minutes when suddenly a shockwave hit us both. AH—*eek eek –eeek-eeek-ah*, the loon emitted his crazylike call, chilling me clear to the toes. The cry was so close and so loud that it seemed to be coming from some place next to me. Again the *Aar-eek, eek, eee-eeek, ah* came, louder than ever this time, like a squealing stuck

pig or child being pierced by some sharp instrument—a wild, fren-
zied cry that sent agonizing shockwaves across the quiet Barrens.
Then the impersonator of those wild screams slipped into view. He
was a red-throat all right: black-white features, reddish throat,
sharp-pointed bill, head nervously swinging in jerks from side to
side, swimming effortlessly in a small pool of water surrounded by
small rocks. I glassed him for a few minutes when again he threw
his head upward and pumped out a frightening Arctic serenade.

For a full hour and a half the loon and the sik-sik and I were
performer and audience. The loon would call, I would glass him,
then a second loon would answer from another part of the lake.
The sik-sik would come up and investigate, blink and pop back
into his den. Finally, I decided to fully expose myself. The action
startled the loon. He jumped up, splashing, and took off for
another part of the lake. Then all was quiet once more. The sik-sik
popped up, winked, fluttered his nose and shot back into his burrow for the last time. By now cramps had developed in my legs
and a disappearing sun told me it was time to leave.

One cannot mention the sik-sik, sometimes referred to as the
Arctic ground squirrel, without pointing out its uniqueness. This
ground-dwelling marmot is one of the few really true hibernators in
North America. One normally thinks of the bears as hibernating
animals, but this is not quite true. Bears don't really hibernate. On
the tundra the Barren Ground grizzly merely goes to sleep in the
coldest part of the winter, but his body temperature remains almost
normal. This is likewise true of the female polar bear when having
her young. She simply finds a nice protected spot along the ice
somewhere and goes into a kind of half sleep; the male polar bear
does not even do this. But the marmot is different. This small
squirrel of the mainland tundra really goes into a deep, almost lifeless torpor for about eight months of the year. During winter its
respiration is very slow, perhaps once every two or three minutes,
and its body temperature comes close to freezing. This low body
heat and slow rate of breathing allows the squirrel to survive because its rate of energy consumption is thereby very low. Lemmings, on the other hand, are not hibernators, but remain active all
winter long in ice crevices, among the rocks and in burrows under
the snow. These rodents maintain a regular normal body temperature all year long. Not the sik-sik. Thus, the marmot is the only
true hibernating mammal in the entire Arctic.

I finally started walking back to camp.

As I moved toward the setting sun over the expanseful tundra I thought about the loon. Why had this bird intrigued me so much? I guess the thing that I enjoy most about the loon is its symbolism. These birds, in general, symbolize certain qualities in nature that many men admire, action which, I suspect, many of us would like to pursue or grasp had we the chance. One of these, I sense, is carfreeness, another is impulsiveness. Unlike most birds that sing or give voice to establish and command a breeding territory, the loon laughs or cries for the sheer joy of laughing, of being free and footloose, of being wingloose in a wild world. Perhaps, more than any other quality, the loon symbolizes and personifies the true wild spirit of nature. A laughing loon on the Arctic Barrens, could anything be more wild?

My experience with these loons was not an earth-shattering event, but it taught me some things about solitude and primeval wildness that I never knew before—that the true wilderness, even though treeless, has a character that touches one deep inside. The plain, everyday loon has an essentiality in nature that is both integral and sublime. Everything seems to have a special place in the Creator's world and I would suspect that the so-called mad loon, which is not a just way of referring to him, has his.

So loons and symbolism go together. I suppose we could live without these strange birds, just as we could live without the whooping cranes or whippoorwills, but at what price? In my book the loon and wildness are one and the same. Both are worth perpetuating, saving. We can't have one without the other. Because all humans at times are loners and because we all need a bit of solitude now and then to keep our sensibilities on an even plain, we cannot allow the loon or what it represents to disappear from our lives.

11
Sojourn to the High Arctic

A year after my caribou sojourns on the Barrens my desire to see the so-called High Arctic became intense. But how does a man of modest means get up into this country—to Baffin Island, Cornwallis Island, and other islands of the Arctic Archipelago?

Well, piece by piece one gets the answers. I found, for example, that there is a commercial airline, Nordair, that flies a regular schedule summer and winter between Montreal, Frobisher Bay, Baffinland, and Resolute Bay in the heart of the Canadian Arctic Archipelago.

For weeks I studied the maps. Resolute is the farthest outpost in the North one can fly to commercially. It is located on Cornwallis Island some five hundred miles north of the Arctic Circle and not much over eight hundred miles from the North Pole.

Frobisher? Resolute? The places sounded intriguing. I would go.

But one just doesn't pack and go to these remote places. You must make prior arrangements with the Canadian Department of Transport if you want a place to stay at both Frobisher and Resolute.

While I wanted a place to stay for a while, I also wanted to camp out, alone, along the Arctic ice pack, so I made arrangements and preparations for both.

The Nordair flight from Montreal to Frobisher Bay is nonstop, a distance of fifteen hundred miles, and it is an all night trip. The plane leaves Montreal at 11:00 P.M. and arrives at Frobisher Bay at dawn.

When you begin seeing daylight over Baffin Island and look down across a vast domain of gray something, you are confused. Is this country all a frozen sea? Are those mountains really covered with ice and snow? You are finally convinced that the country you see is really mountains covered with ice and snow and that it must be a hellishly cold place in this no-man's-land.

The country approaching Frobisher Bay is fiercely wild. When the plane begins letting down you see mostly ice and snow and frozen sea. Interspersed between large bodies of sea ice are snow-covered mountains and much desolation. For a long time in the re-vealing dawn there is not the slightest hint of civilization and you begin wondering if anything resembling a settlement will ever show up. But a small settlement finally shows up and you land and get out. It is cold but you are happy because you are alive.

The danger in flying to Frobisher is probably not this great. Part of the anxiety one feels comes from the early morning purple gray-ness of the landscape. But once down on terra firma, the picture eases somewhat, yet the ruggedness of the landscape doesn't change. There is so much rock and ice around Frobisher that you think this is the high Arctic already. Yet you're still one hundred miles south of the Arctic Circle and a long, long way from the real high Arctic, like Ellesmere Island.

There is no great fanfare at Frobisher. You either have some business here, go to town in a dusty taxi, or shuttle in a large, jeep-like truck over to the Department of Transport billets.

I stayed several days at the government billets, ate my own ra-tions in my room, walked around a great deal, and purchased a fishing license at the R. C. M. P. office.

I had the embarrassing episode of being chased off the airport grounds by a none-too-friendly official. It came about through Jim Stevens, a local man with the utility company who tried to be help-ful. Jim works to provide the power in Frobisher and collects the garbage. I met him casually the first day and asked him about Arc-tic char fishing. He told me to hike to the Sylvia Grinnel River but to take a shortcut across the end of the airport runway. "Then it's only a mile or two to the river. Saves you much walking," he said.

The next morning I started out, lugging a full pack, camera, fishing tackle, etc. No sooner had I gotten well past the end of the airstrip when a car came racing across the field, stopped, and a man waved frantically.

"Where in hell do you think *you're* going?" a gruff-looking man yelled as I finally approached. "You're off limits. Do you want to get killed?"

There hadn't been a plane on the field all day, but this man was raving mad. It was only because of my past experience with angry men that I was able to calm this fellow down and explain what I was trying to do. The man finally eased off a bit but refused me permission to proceed on the short cut. He then got back into his car and dashed away.

"Well," I thought, "this is some treatment of an American by the friendly Canadians, and not even offering a lift all the way back to the billets." I was quite chagrined, for in all my travels in Canada I had never been treated so unkindly and unceremoniously before.

Later, I mentioned the incident to Jim Stevens and he seemed puzzled and shrugged it off, saying that this guy was merely trying to show his self-importance. As it was, not a single plane landed on the gravel airstrip all the remainder of the day. The episode, however, failed to dampen my spirits and after some four miles of hiking, I finally made it to the river.

The Sylvia Grinnell is a big, treacherous, cold river, with its source obviously somewhere in the melting ice and snow high country to the southwest. I climbed down a series of mean-looking cliffs, over ledges and huge boulders and eventually got to a rocky ledge along the river's edge. Here it seemed safe to cast. For a good half hour I worked the green-looking big river, trying to give my red devil spoon all the life I knew, but not a tap came. Then I remembered that someone had mentioned the rapids and immediately my mind was made up. I would gradually work up there and fish along the way.

The going was the toughest I had ever experienced. I took turns scaling huge rocks, fishing, and photographing. Finally after two hours I got to the rapids—two rapids, in fact, one large and one a bit smaller—and I could easily see that I would be lucky to make the lesser of the two. The river here is a good three hundred yards wide, swift and noisy, and strewn with rocks and huge boulders around which treacherous eddies formed. I cast into a likely looking pool below the smaller falls and to my surprise got a strike and felt a fish on. After a bit of maneuvering I pulled in my first Arctic char. It was a small one, about sixteen inches, silvery, almost like a coho salmon, but slimmer and more streamlined. I tried hard to pick up more of these beautiful fish but one was all that luck would give me on this trip.

I took the fish to a small cafe in town and persuaded a lady there to cook it for me. She didn't mind. In fact, she was delighted to do it and didn't even charge me for doing it. Such accomodations are rare in the United States where most restaurants won't cook your fish even if you pay them.

The fish was beautifully pinkish when cooked and delectable, as most trout are when cooked fresh. That evening on my way to the billets I was picked up by a couple in a car who had been to the river. They had three very large char, one of which would easily weigh twelve pounds and was well over two and a half feet long. It was enough to urge me to stay another day or two and try my luck again, but my plane was leaving for Resolute the next morning. The Arctic char of the Sylvia Grinnell River would have to await my return visit some other day in mid-August. I vowed to return.

The clerk at the Department of Transport where I was staying said I should be ready at 5:30 A.M. to check out and get to the airport. I was ready, along with a truckload of others and were driven to the hangar as scheduled. But there things came to a dead halt. About twenty heavily clad men and women were in the waiting room, all sleepy and very quiet. No one said much and no explanation of any delays was given by the man who was checking the baggage. Yet when our Constellation wasn't starting up it was perfectly obvious that something was wrong.

Curiosity finally got the best of me and I inquired about the trouble. I thought perhaps it was the plane but it wasn't. The trouble was the weather at Resolute. Fog. We would have to wait until it lifted—an hour maybe, perhaps longer. As it turned out it was *much* longer. In fact it was about one o'clock in the afternoon when we finally sensed that we were to board. Again, no one said anything. There was no announcement. Everyone just started for the plane and got aboard.

I asked the stewardess, a French-looking girl, if this was normal and she said, "Yes," very sweetly and I went past her and took a window seat. Soon all four motors were warmed up, the doors closed and we began moving. We lumbered over the gravel runway like some giant bird, turned, felt the motors go into a roar, and took off into the North Wind. The captain swung a little left over

Frobisher Bay, picked up flashes of wet-looking clouds, and then veered the craft into the northwest sky.

When he finally gained our cruising altitude there were a few cloud openings and we could see great patches of ice and snow below. Every few minutes the view through the clouds changed. I was deeply struck by the ruggedness and fierceness of the landscape.

Baffin Island is an enormous place, cold, bleak, and incredibly wild. It is the largest island in the Canadian Arctic Archipelago and the fifth largest in the world. Its total length exceeds one thousand miles and its width varies from two hundred to five hundred miles. Only by flying over it can one get some appreciation of its size.

And little is known of this immense island. Even geographers are not in agreement on its principal physical features and climate. Much of the country is a plateau with ridges running up to three

View of bleak Cornwallis Island, in the Canadian Arctic Archipelago.

thousand feet and some mountain peaks rising to over eight thousand feet. Flying over the treacherous land one sees many glaciers and, along its very uneven coastline, numerous bays and fjords.

Martin Frobisher explored the southern region of the island in the years 1576-78 and later, in 1616, William Baffin, for whom the island was named, explored the northern part. I was told by an informed-looking northerner on the plane that about three thousand Eskimos live on this island, plus some whites who are mostly government people, Hudson Bay Company employees, and mine company prospectors.

The flight over Baffin Island to Resolute Bay is largely over the most rugged part of the island, and on clear days hundreds of cliffs, lakes, and thousands of lakelets can be seen. The largest lakes are Nettling and Amadjack. From the air they look like frozen seas. There is so much ice and snow on Baffin that one wonders at times if he's not over the interior of Greenland.

Most of the ice seen from the air is pack ice, a dangerous coastal, loose kind of ice in the summer which all pilots fear and try to avoid. Our Constellation, however, took all this in stride and we flew over endless miles of it. One can easily understand how the early explorers, like Baffin, Frobisher, and Franklin must have had a treacherous time of it in this bleak unchartered world.

After more than five hours of flying time, most of the passengers began getting a little restless. According to our watches we were supposed to be landing.

When we finally started down at Resolute the country outside was nothing but rough-looking clouds. We kept dropping lower until everyone began glancing about, nervously. Could the captain be having trouble finding the small landing strip in this vast, shrouded Arctic? Lower and lower we went until I finally spotted a break in the clouds. We seemed dangerously low over the land. There were snow patches on it and it looked just as bleak as the land of Baffin we had just left. Then some orange-colored buildings came into view and we skimmed over them at about three hundred feet, and then on over much ice, obviously Resolute Bay. The pilot made a very wide, slow turn, banking over an all-white sea, then turned more and more and finally nosed the plane in for a landing. We hit hard gravel but it was a smooth touchdown and I breathed easier.

A dozen or so bearded people, all with rough-looking parkas and

General view of Cornwallis Island.

heavy coats greeted us. Some were definitely Eskimos and everyone was wearing sunglasses although the weather was cloudy and blustery. The temperature felt about 35°F. We disembarked, waited around for awhile, and then joined a strange procession of moving feet toward a group of orange-red buildings some three hundred yards away. It seemed to me as if this was one of the most wild and desolate places in the world and landing here in a commercial airliner appeared a bit out of place.

One stays at the Resolute base camp by prior agreement or he must shift for himself in a camp-out. I came prepared for both. I felt lucky that my first few days of orientation would be in the barracks. I had a small, comfortable, warm room, and was next door to the Musk Ox Inn, a large building that houses most of the service facilities: mess hall, laundry room, recreation room, dispensary, and a PX bar that was open evenings. Several other buildings made up the base complex, housing the weather bureau, post office, library, and a lone R.C.M.P. office with one mountie who was away on a stretcher case. They said he had to take a patient to Edmonton via a private chartered small plane. The sick man had gone berserk because of the incredible loneliness at the base.

The workers here numbered about eighty men, some wore beards. The social gathering place is the mess hall where one can get coffee and cookies at any time.

"They feed us well here," a chap sitting next to me at my first coffee session said. "They have to try to keep the men content or things could be bad."

"What do you all do here?" I asked. "Oh, we all work. Some keep the airfield open. Others scrape the roads. Some cook and clean up, all kinds of jobs, plumbers, carpenters." And then came, "What do you do?"

I told my friend that I was here on vacation, or as you say in Canada, "on a bit of a holiday."

Several other men were listening intently to our conversation and

Broad view of Cornwallis Island from a ridge.

Migrating Barren Ground caribou (closeup).

Flowering Arctic tundra near Churchill.

laughed, "Holiday!" It was funny. But soon I explained that I was also doing a bit of Arctic research, writing, and taking pictures. This seemed to make a little more sense and from then on I was accepted as one of them.

The country around Resolute is bleak. There is no other way to explain it, just plain, down to earth bleak. And the weather, in the summer, all August, they tell you, is foul. This means that the wind is blowing and it is either raining or misting or sleeting. The time to see Resolute, they say, is in the winter and early spring. Then it is beautifully clear, cold, and mostly white.

12
The Phantom Goliath of the Frozen North

A few days after my arrival at Resolute Bay, I hitched a Bombardier (half-track snow vehicle) ride to an Eskimo settlement some five miles away. I wanted to see the village in leisure, talk with natives, and take pictures.

The settlement is located along the edge of Resolute Bay overlooking a wide open frozen bay. The bay is only open for five weeks in late July and August. Back at camp I was told that this was a relatively new settlement, one that the Canadian government had set up when they brought the Eskimos down from Gris Fjord, on Ellesmere Island. There were too many Eskimos there and they were starving. Around a hundred natives were brought down and given modest new cottages and offered jobs at the Resolute base.

It was grayish cold, wintry, so typical of this strange country and I saw few people around. Where the natives were was hard to figure out. There were several groups of huskies tied up on the ice and when they saw my unusual figure with cameras dangling about me, they let out a series of mournful howls.

One gets the impression in wandering about such a place that he is an intruder, and indeed he is. The Eskimos belong in this northland but a white man does not. If the white man has contributed anything to these marvelously independent people, some observers say, it is only disease and degradation. The real Eskimo native has good teeth and perfect normal vision but when they get mixed up

Resolute Bay, Cornwallis Island.

with whites they are seen eating candy, developing bad teeth, and wearing eyeglasses. At the Resolute base camp nearly all of the Eskimos wear very dark sunglasses and the strangest mixture of clothes—blue denim, Army shirts, and jackets, all kinds of boots including Wellingtons; their parkas are embroidered with colorful trimmings and have collars lined with wolf fur.

I came to the Eskimo village mostly to learn about the polar bear. Draped around a dozen cottages, some of which were painted with hideous colors, were lines of drying clothes and a number of skins. Paul Katorosky, a game official from Fort Smith, told me at base camp that this group of Eskimos had taken a hundred polar bear this past spring, mostly by about twenty-five hunters. A good skin with a fine head brings about $150 from buyers from the fur companies, like the Hudson Bay Company, or from workers or visitors at the base. Polar bear rugs or wall skins for some reason unknown to me, because they always seem to smell, continue to be popular.

I met an Eskimo finally at one house and tried to engage him in conversation. He looked up at me through his sunglasses, pipe hanging from the corner of his mouth, grinned and drooled through his teeth but said nothing.

"May I take your picture?" I asked (one must always do this up here), and he just gurgled and hissed good naturedly through his teeth. Finally he said *Amashook,* which means polar bear and pointed to the skins in his back yard. I said "No thank you," I did not want to buy any.

My new found friend was trying to start his Skidoo, a small snowmobile with runners, and kept pulling and pulling on the starter cord. I thought after a while that he would drop from exhaustion. But no, he just kept on pulling. These small people are incredibly strong and have tremendous energy. This man was trying to carry out a load of garbage to his dogs on the ice and his machine was the way to pull the sled. I finally left the man in a bit of a puzzle because the box of garbage on the sled wasn't so big and I thought the simplest thing to do was to carry it out to the dogs.

That evening, Paul Kartorosky came down to the village school for a meeting and talk with the Eskimo hunters. I was invited to attend and see what I could learn.

"You are taking too many polar bear," Paul said to the group through a young Eskimo interpreter. "I want to talk to you about polar bear."

Paul pointed out that there was international sentiment for complete polar bear protection and that if the Canadian Eskimos were not to be deprived of their right to hunt polar bears they would have to consider accepting an annual quota—fifty bears for the Resolute area.

As the evening wore on I became engaged in a conversation with a young Eskimo, Uni, who spoke a little English. He said he was sixteen but looked twelve.

"Have you ever killed a polar bear?" I asked.

"Oh, yes, many," came the reply.

"And when did you kill your first?"

"Long, long time ago," he came back quickly.

I had no reason to doubt the lad. Yet a boy of nine or ten killing a polar bear on the ice was indeed a remarkable feat.

The polar bear is considered as the great white ghost of the Arctic. He is a formidable creature, long in body, short of tail, and exceedingly swift afoot on land and in the water. A large male can go well over half a ton and some truly large goliaths reach fifteen hundred pounds or more.

Later in the evening I asked one of the experienced hunters how close he gets to the bear when he shoots and he replied, translated, "Not very close."

"Are you ever scared?" I asked. He grinned and said, "Oh yes, very very scared—always."

I learned that the Eskimos hunt only the "man bear" or bull bear, since it is illegal to take the sows and cubs. They know they're following a man bear because the track is huge—twelve by eighteen inches—and it is usually alone. Whenever a smaller track appears with the big tracks, or is accompanied by still smaller tracks, the Eskimo hunters turn away. This they know to be a mother bear with young.

The polar bear is the Arctic's largest water-land denizen. *Courtesy A. W. Ambler, National Audubon Society.*

How do Eskimos hunt down a polar bear? I got the story in broken English from one of the hunters and it goes something like this:

"Take dog team and grub. Take son, he help make snow house. Follow big track. . .one hour. . .one day. Night we sleep in snow house. Sleep. Dogs outside, smell too much in snow house. Morning we hunt track again. Cover many miles. Maybe track get hot. Dogs wild. Cut two dogs loose from sled. . .they chase bear. Bear not afraid, runs, stops to fight. We come. I shoot the bear, he runs. . .real mad now. Can kill dogs. I shoot again. Big fight. Bear slaps dogs. But we get him."

I thanked my Eskimo friend for his story and Paul and I said good-bye and left for Resolute. "You know," Paul said, as we bounded over the road in a Bombardier for camp, "these Eskimos are something. The bear are getting scarce. I'd like to teach them how to hunt musk-ox for sport. The bears need to be left alone; the musk-ox could stand some thinning."

The hunted polar bear is himself a master hunter. Confined largely to the polar ice pack and subsisting mostly on seal, he has developed a remarkable talent for catching seal. To understand how the phantom goliath of the frozen north does this one must know something of how a seal survives in the polar north, especially in winter.

Being mammals, most seals can stay under water only a few minutes, on rare occasions up to seven, even twenty minutes. Then they must surface to expel used air and take in several mouthfuls of oxygen. In the summer months when the ice pack is sufficiently broken up and ice and water intermingle, the seals have no problem. The animals simply surface wherever there is open water. Frequently they climb aboard an ice pan to rest or bask in the sun or nap. It is when surfacing or napping that the seal is most vulnerable to the bear. The white ghost simply sneaks up on an unsuspecting seal and administers the *coup de grace.*

But seal hunting in the winter is quite different. As soon as the polar sea begins to freeze up in September the seal selects a favorite feeding ground and pokes its muzzle through the ice in several places, sometimes as many as eight or ten places, and continually keeps them open as the ice thickens. Soon these air holes take on the form of inverted funnels while, at the same time, a mound or hummock or two is built up from freezing blow-hole water on the surface. These mounds, called *aglo* by the Eskimos, are the objects the polar bear seeks out. Taking a watchful position alongside an *aglo,* the polar bear waits and listens. Sometimes he scratches the ice with his three-inch front claws, hoping the curious seal will come to the blow-hole to investigate. If it does, one mighty swat of a front foot comes down upon it and savage teeth tear into the seal and its whole form is pulled up through broken ice, bodily.

Arctic seal—the main food item of the polar bear.

When the ice is very thick the bear has a more difficult time of it and must devour as much of the seal as it can in the *aglo*. Mostly, however, the bear seeks out the larger cracks in the ice. Hiding behind a pressure ridge, creeping forward on padded feet with only black eyes and nose showing, it dashes suddenly here and there after a surfacing seal.

At Resolute there was lots of talk of polar bears. Now and then one was reported along the ice-packed coast some seven miles away. The more I thought about it, the more I thought that a camp-out in this area might give me a chance to see one of these goliaths.

So I packed my one-man Arctic tent, sleeping bag, and some food, and started out. Several of the camp men I talked to thought it was risky to go out there alone—and without even a gun. But the adventurous do such things and I paid no heed to the warnings. The hike took several hours and when I reached the pack ice, I was

Resolute Bay, Cornwallis Island.

The author's tent along the Arctic ice pack on Cornwallis Island.

ready for a long rest. As I sat on a rock looking across the ice I suddenly became uneasy. Yes, maybe it was foolish coming out here alone.

I pitched my tent and tried to forget all bad thoughts. I was very tired from the hard day and crawled into my sleeping bag and tried to rest. I have found, however, that when one is under tension, slumber does not come. Although I was quite certain that I was not in any great danger, I worried a little about a marauding polar bear. These animals do move along the edge of the sea ice at times. Moreover, I couldn't help for a moment to think of the large painting in the United States Weather Bureau office in Resolute that showed a great polar bear hovering over a wounded man on the polar ice and devouring him. What if such a bear did come sniffing by my tent; what defense would I have? Then I remembered that it was Jim Larsen, veteran worker at the base camp, who said, "You know I wouldn't go out there without a rifle if I were you. You never can tell." Then I thought of the size of the

polar bear skin in the camp mess hall and the thickness of the
bear's skull and that my sole weapon was a scout knife in my pants
pocket. I tried dismissing these thoughts and rolled over and started
counting sheep.

But the sound of moving polar ice was not conducive to sleep.
The periodic low booming tumultuous sounds came like deep bangs
of thunder. Sometimes a great cake near shore would give way and
crash against another mass of thick ice. The ice pans were five and
six feet thick and when they collided the ground beneath me shook.
Once several long-tailed jaegers flew over head and hollered, obviously distraught at seeing a strange orange tent below them. Other
than the ice and birds there was almost no sound—no wind, or
rain, or sleet. This was rare, for Cornwallis naturally has much
foul weather.

Then my mind wandered off to Franklin and his men—what
could have ever happened to them. More than a hundred and
twenty two years earlier he had been here, or near here, bent on
finding the Northwest Passage. Sir John Franklin came with two
ships and 128 officers, camped on some small island between
Cornwallis and Devon, buried three of his men who died, and then
sailed away. He was never to be seen or heard from again.

Then I thought of the mountie, two Eskimos, and their dog
teams, who only this very spring had taken off from Greenland
across the sea ice, over frozen Baffin, to Resolute. They subsisted
almost entirely from the ice and land (mostly seal and polar bear).
That was a feat—and they survived.

So sleep was out of the question. I zipped open my sleeping
bag, pulled on my boots and went out into the midnight evening
glow. Such silence. The scene was bewitching. All was deathly
stillness. For the first time in my life I felt the full measure of silence, that feeling of complete, utter solitude; loneliness, no, but
just plain aloneness and I shivered to it. I put on my parka and
went scouting along the sea ice. A walk might do me good and
take the tenseness out of my nerves.

Not far from my tent I discovered two sprung steel traps. They
must have been left by Eskimo trappers or floated in on breaking
ice in seasons past. Rusty and attached to small boards they were
in working condition, so I picked them up and took them along.
Then I found a wooden plank, a 2 × 4 about three feet long, with
one sharp end. It too, could have floated in from somewhere on the
ice. Traps and plank in hand, I went to work. I set the steel traps

in front of my tent and fashioned a club-axe out of the plank by tying to it a large rock. The traps would do little except warn me or pinch the toes of a polar bear and might serve as a source of discouragement. And were a bear to really come and poke his head into my quarters, I could at least nail him with that club. It all seemed a little ridiculous, since surely a polar bear's appearance was remote. But it was enough to give me that extra confidence I needed to go to sleep.

Sometime after midnight, really midnight-daylight, I awoke to the flapping of my tent and the sound of wind and rain. Once again the foul Arctic weather had set in and I was getting it full blast. I went outside several times to tighten the tent ropes and pile more rocks around the metal tent pins, each time getting drenched by the wind-blasted rain. At one point through the muffled roar of the wind across the ice, I thought I heard the deep-throated bellow of a polar bear. Could it really be, or was it the echo of a tied husky at the Eskimo village some ten miles away? The Arctic polar bear goes ashore sometime in the Arctic Archipelago, let's out an occasional muffled roar, but normally is a shy beast and is seldom seen. Yet I felt satisfied that I heard a real ice bear, and was elated. But shivers swept down my spine. How far away could he be? Then I thought of the wolves I heard in James Bay and how silly it was to be afraid. Would the phantom goliath of the frozen north call again and could I try to describe it in words? I grabbed my journal and pen and waited.

But not another bear call came. The sounds were of elemental nature only, the wind, the sleet, the pelting raindrops across my tent now filled with at least a gallon of water. For ten long minutes I strained each ear but no animal sounds came. There are some things in the natural world that one is treated to only once, and I know now, it is such an experience that is most impressionable and the longest lasting.

Two hours later, tired, wet, cold, hungry, but buoyant in heart and whistling to myself in the Arctic sleet, I scrambled out of my abode and broke camp. I packed a wet pack and started hiking for base camp with the North Wind pushing me all the way.

I was disappointed in not seeing a polar bear but satisfied I had heard one. That was good enough for me.

13
Oomingmak at Last

Cornwallis is a desolate island in the Arctic Archipelago and the wildlife there is not plentiful. Mosquitoes may occur here but during my stay on the island, I saw none. The summer climate is too cold. On one ridge, however, I did see a small gray moth. But a young man, John Penny, who worked for the Tower Foundation——the outfit that runs the base camp at Resolute Bay—would disagree on the wildlife. He kept telling me of the abundance of musk-ox, especially at a place where a British team of scientists were conducting Arctic ecological studies. The distance out to where the musk-ox were supposed to be so common was about seven miles and he offered me a ride out to that area in a snowmobile. I was to be ready the next time the researchers went out to check their climatological gear and soil plots.

"Oh, they're all around the place," he would often say, "and you can almost pet them." But he gave a half wink to his friends when he said *almost*.

The next morning I got word that Penny was going out. There were several others besides the research team who wanted a ride——two bearded soil scientists, Lorna Dubliqy, the wife of Dick Dubliqy who worked as a pilot for the Atlas Air Lines, Ltd., her visiting brother, Reggie, and myself.

The snowmobile, called a Bombardier, was no traditional small snow vehicle but a large sort of a half track and geared for very rough country. John Penny had given instructions to the driver where to drop all of us extras off. The going was fair for about five miles and then got horribly bumpy. The next two or three miles was one great bounce after another.

The vehicle finally halted in a wild no-man's-land and all but the driver and the research team disembarked. "This is where they were," the driver said. "You'll just have to look for them."

We glanced around the barren land, saw only snowbanks here and there and said very little. Nothing but wasteland greeted us. Then several of us started walking toward some high ground, the two soil scientists in the lead, the rest of us following. Meanwhile the bombardier moved off and disappeared near a large lake and was not to be seen again that day.

We hiked briskly up a long, windswept ridge toward a wide snowbank, then down a ravine, across a swollen stream, and up onto another long ridge. If this was going to be the pace, I was soon going to drop back. While the rest traveled lightly, I was heavily weighed down by a 16 mm Bolex motion picture camera

Snowbanks on Cornwallis Island.

and tripod, and three still cameras—a 4 × 5 speed Graphic, a Rol-leiflex, and a 35 mm Rico camera for slides.

We had traveled about a mile and a half when the two soil scien-tists stopped. "They're on the other ridge," said one of them nonchalantly. . ."way over there."

Two black and white forms loomed on the skyline more than three-quarters of a mile away. We rested, glassed them, and took a few pictures. In a few minutes we took after them. They were ob-viously two renegade bull musk-ox and wanted no quarter from us, for they were moving away rapidly. We followed them for a mile or so and then lost them in the ridge country. They outdistanced us easily. The soil scientists kept up the pursuit but whether they ever got very close to them, I will never know. Slowly the bleak Arctic landscape absorbed their human forms until nothing of them re-mained. I never saw them again.

Reggie, Lorna, and I sat down on some rocks near a snowbank and talked about musk-ox. What wonderful animals they were,

Bleak terrain of Arctic tundra near Resolute Bay.

how marvelously adapted to live in this inhospitable country, how old in point of time.

Strangely enough the musk-ox persists only in the New World, mostly in Arctic Canada and Greenland. Several hundred are found in Alaska, on Nunivak Island, where they were reintroduced some years back after having been exterminated in Alaska about the turn of the century. Overhunting is said to have been responsible.

Reggie wondered how many musk-ox there were and I told him of my conversation with the game superintendent from Ft. Smith. Paul gave me what he thought might be reasonable population figures:

Estimated No.

CANADA	
Bathurst Island	
Melville Island	1,100
Axel Heilberg Island	1,000
Ellesmere Island	1,000
Banks Island	4,000
Victoria Island	1,000
Cornwallis Island	300
Misc. Arch. Islands	200
Mainland (barren grounds)	700
(1,000 of which are estimated	7,000
in the Thelon Game Preserve)	
Canada total	16,300
ALASKA	500
GREENLAND	5,000
Grand Total	
	21,800

These figures, of course, are only educated guesses. Paul thought they were conservative. Some biologists however think they're high.

One thing is certain: the species is definitely one of the most remarkably adapted hooved mammals on earth. It has unbelievable ability to withstand bitter Arctic temperatures, a scant food supply, and long, dark days, weeks, and months of terrible weather. So persistent is the musk-ox that some of their kind are found on a sea island only 350 miles from the North Pole. The musk-ox is a unique mammal. A thick, long-haired wooly coat covers the entire body, and this covering plus heavy layers of fat, and the animal's ability to paw for ground plants with sharp hooves through ice and

Icebergs in the eastern Arctic.

snow, makes the musk-ox a very special creature. No other large land mammal lives further north than this throwback to the Ice Age, a feature that has endeared him to many who know and love wildlife. How the animal can withstand the bitter void of Arctic winters when temperatures are well below zero degrees F much of the time is a mystery. Yet these animals hold their own, even are increasing in numbers. While "ole shag," as he is sometimes called, has no enemies outside of man and, perhaps on rare occasions, the Arctic wolf, life in an extreme environment takes its toll.

The musk-ox does not appear to be dangerous but like most wild creatures is unpredictable. These beasts must be treated with respect and left unprovoked or the exception to the rule can spell harm or tragedy to the molester. In ninety-nine cases out of a hundred the musk-ox will flee a human being. When unable to escape, it quickly forms into its defensive ring, heads out, rumps in, calves well back into the center. As the intruder approaches the whole ring will sway back and forth, the big beasts stomping the

ground, pawing, snorting and spewing defiance and hot breath
from their nostrils, like dragons.

Sometimes a bull or a big cow will lunge forward to half its
length, as if to charge, but it quickly backs into its former position
and continues its defense.

The size of these animals is amazing. Even at a distance they
look imposing. Large, full-grown bulls will weigh up to eight
hundred, nine hundred, even one thousand pounds and stand five
feet at the shoulder, thus a large bull makes a formidable bulk of
powerful flesh and bone. Even the lighter cows are no small
beasts, and when with calf can be dangerous.

There is one reasonable reliable instance of a musk-ox attack on
a human in Greenland which I cite as having happened, although I
personally did not know the individual. He was a lieutenant in the
American Air Force on weather duty, when one day in his spare
time he wandered away from his base with a dog to paint a particular landscape. As he worked away on canvas a colleague at a dis-

Musk-ox besieged by wolves.

tant outpost, more than a mile away, saw a musk-ox charge him. Shouting did little good because the distance was too great.

The officer, hearing something unusual rushing toward him, wheeled, grabbed his rifle and tried to shoot. In the excitement the cartridge jammed. The dog, however, came to the rescue, barked interference for just enough time so that the lieutenant could clear his gun, shoot, and kill the animal. It was a big cow musk-ox. Tracks later revealed it had come over the ridge where it was protecting a small calf.

Wildlife biologists are forever warning people to leave wild animals alone, not to pick up young, and simply not to trust wild animals. One can never categorize traits as "never" in wild animals. This is because animal behavior, like behavior in humans, sometimes deviates from the norm. Mentality, age, sickness, ailments such as sore feet, mouths, or old bullet wounds, all contribute their share to patterns of unusual behavior. So the best that can be said is that under normal conditions an animal will not do this or that.

But what about the musk-ox we were following on Cornwallis? Was there any use going further? Reggie thought it might be worthwhile to cross the next ravine and climb the distant ridge where our two bulls had disappeared an hour before. Lorna and I agreed and we started on our trek again. An hour later we gained the main promontory but saw no sign of musk-ox. We rested. Once more I took pictures and ran off some movie footage. Lorna decided she had had enough and announced she would turn back and hike the eight or ten miles back to the camp. I was a bit surprised at the announcement but she thought nothing of it. She threw back her parka and started off.

Meanwhile, Reggie and I decided to combine talents and resources and see if we could come upon a musk-ox still, he attempting to drive while I would angle off and photograph.

"I'll make a great semicircle around that long hill and if I see any, I'll try to press them toward you. Suppose we rendezvous down around North Lake in a couple of hours?"

The scheme was agreeable but the results were not productive. In three miles of walking and scanning and studying everything suspicious, not a thing turned up. We got together on top of an esker on the shore of North Lake and Reg pulled out a sandwich. "I'll share it with you. It's all I have, plus some dried up old raisins, what say?"

Searching for musk-ox on Cornwallis Island.

How he knew that I had not brought along any lunch I will never know. Intuition, I guess. Anyway, a half sandwich and old raisins never tasted so good in all my life.

Reg and I separated after our skimpy meal, he hiking back toward the base at Resolute while I trekked over to inspect Dr. Hannel's study area. The latter proved strangely interesting. Micro-climatology is quite a science and is shedding light on how plants and animals are able to survive in the Arctic.

Dr. Hannell and his assistant were reading and recording data in one of two tents in the study section. "We're trying to find out the effect of soil temperatures at various levels and on soil treated on the surface with white as well as black powders." His cabbage plants and eighteen hills of potatoes under polyethyline tarp were "doing well."

After a hospitality of tea and some amiable conversation, the two scientists went back to work and I went on to photograph some of the scant plant growth.

An Arctic research team on Cornwallis Island.

"By the way, Dr. Hannel," I put in, "how's the lake and stream water for drinking?" The genial man with a decidedly British accent hesitated for a moment, then looked back at me, saying, "Oh, very well. . .purer, safer, and better than gin, you know."

I was intrigued by the musk-ox sign about, clusters of dark, brown-black droppings, all round balls averaging ⅝ to ¾ of an inch in diameter. Every hundred feet or so a mass of droppings showed up and I began getting encouraged that I might yet see a musk-ox.

What kept intriguing me was the scant food. Could this seemingly spare vegetation, a little mound of saxifrage here, a blanket of brown moss there, or a lone prostrate willow flowing over a flat limestone somewhere, could these few scrawny plants sustain such large animals? Apparently so. There was no other conclusion to draw. Surely then these strange plants must have a high concentration of food value, for not only does the musk-ox thrive on them in the summer but must subsist on them all during the long winter months.

About 5:00 P.M. a plane came over North Lake, circled, then flew on. In ten minutes, it was back again, once more circling. I waved as it dropped down, skimming a nearby ridge and, to my surprise, landed. It was Lorna and her pilot husband, Dick Dubliqy.

"Want a lift," hollered Lorna, as the plane's motor stopped. "Long ways back to camp, you know."

It was a pleasant and unexpected surprise and I couldn't help but accept the invitation. It was the first time I had been picked up by a plane in the Arctic without even hitchhiking.

"We scouted the country ahead," Dick said, "and there is no musk-ox in sight. Guess this just wasn't your day."

We piled into the plane and took off. In a few minutes Lorna pointed: "There's Reggie, let's pick him up, too."

We did. It was a pleasant bit of helpfulness and cooperation in the Arctic.

No sooner had we landed at Resolute when Dick looked at the rarely clearing western sky, reflected for a moment, and turned to me, saying, "I don't know what goes with the game man but if you see him, tell him we can go to Melville—tonight."

I was a bit puzzled by what appeared to be a lack of coordination between the Atlas Air Service, Ltd.'s office and its pilots. At any rate, when I saw Paul Kartorowsky and gave him the message, he was fit to be tied. "All day long I wait for the Atlas office to call and all of a sudden one of the pilots in the field sends word he's ready to go. Oh, these Arctic bush pilots!"

That's how it is. When the weather breaks in this country things start happening. Word spreads quickly. In less than an hour we had had our supper, Paul had rounded up his Eskimo team, and, bag and baggage, we began assembling it at the air strip by the single-engined Otter that was to take his party to Melville Island, some four hundred miles to the northwest. Paul and his Eskimo crew were going to Melville to shoot some game, maybe caribou and musk-ox. Paul had instructions to teach the Eskimos how to hunt for sport—that is, how to guide visiting hunters to big game. Instead of the natives killing all the game themselves perhaps they could be taught how to lead hunting parties to game and make more money that way. The total game quota from the area would be the same.

"Unless the pilot says he can't take all of us or we are overloaded," Paul said to me, "I'd like for you to come along. Too bad, though, you do not have the time to stay with us on Melville. Lots of game there. You'd like it."

I replied that I felt really fortunate in just going and coming right back with the pilot, a stroke of luck I hadn't counted on.

Dick Dubliqy remained silent as he saw all the gear and supplies going aboard the plane, and seven people yet to board. But we apparently made the grade. We were overloaded but the Otter pulled off the ground, climbed slowly at first, then gradually gained altitude over the ice. Reg sat up in front beside Dick and I took the first seat behind him. Paul sat in the cabin with his five Eskimos. The stocky, small natives just sat there, implacably and motionless, peering out the dirty windows. They are an emotionless people and seem to have some of the qualities of the Orientals.

For a long time we flew over ice, great endless stretches of it, mile upon mile, its patterns changing continually. Here and there great cracks appeared, some taking on incredible length and straight as an arrow. Dick kept in radio contact with his Atlas base back at Resolute. Most of the time it was Weldy Phipps's wife who maintains contact with the pilots.

Now and then small barren islands showed up amidst the ice and Dick stayed close to them, and for good reason. There is a period in midsummer when the sea ice is treacherous and landing on it can be suicidal. These bush pilots know it and stay close to land where their large, balloon-tired wheels give them a reasonably safe landing. There is no problem in the winter or fall or late spring when the sea ice is safe. Then the pilots can land either with wheels or on skis. The skis are retractable and give the pilot considerable versatility in take-offs and landings.

After an hour of seeing mostly black ice, a large land mass appeared, the beginning of Bathurst Island. Like Cornwallis, it is essentially a flat, raw, island of sand and gravel and limestone. We flew across several ridges, perhaps clearing them at 360 or 400 feet. They were windswept and completely barren, a land that nature seemingly forgot. In places the terrain opened up great vistas of low, wet ground, brown in shade and twisting with streams and rivulets. All the water was snow water. Here and there we could make out long windrows of snow and gray water gushing from them.

We saw little wildlife although Dick kept pointing out something to Reggie. My eyes are notoriously poor with central vision gone, and even with bincoulars I have a hard time picking up common wildlife, thus there may have been more on the ground than what I was seeing.

Bathurst is perhaps 150 miles long by 175 miles wide, and in a heavily loaded, single-engine Otter, one does not cross it quickly. As we swung over the northwestern section of the island, Dick kept studying the western sky, reporting what he saw over the radio. There was a purple cast to the horizon and a low cloud cover began slowing up.

Suddenly Dick spotted something on the ground and hollered, "Caribou!"

Everyone looked down on the spot. Below a dozen or more animals were running over the rough terrain. At fifteen hundred feet they seemed like gray-white stampeding ghosts, scurrying in every direction and making excellent speed.

Paul said they were Peary caribou, a distinct subspecies that is common in the Canadian Archipelago.

After another look at the western horizon, Dick shook his head. He called back to Paul, "Fog. Can't make Melville. We'll have to land here on Bathurst."

Paul agreed and repeated the disappointing message to an Eskimo interpreter. All of us accepted the decision. Surely it was better to be alive on Bathurst than dead on Melville. All because of a "white-out."

Dick studied his map, looked over the entire horizon, and then turned the plane slowly northward. The ominous fog on our left was a solid sheet of gray and began obscuring everything behind it. But we were angling away from it and soon felt ourselves going down. Dick spotted a familiar great river valley and was following it apparently to some kind of a landing place. How we could land in this desolate land with rough rocks all around us was beyond me.

We kept dropping. Soon we were sailing overland at only a few hundred feet. The rocky ground looked too rugged for comfort. Then Dick leveled off and flew over smaller and smaller beds of gravel and some level ground and I commenced to feel better. It was a good landing, slow, bouncy but the big tires took it well and we were glad.

Our landing at Bathurst Island wasn't the smoothest touchdown in the world. With rocks and gravel strewn all about and not even

Musk-ox herd in defense ring on Bathurst Island.

a semblance of a runway in sight, I thought Dick did pretty well. And no sooner had our Otter slowed down and come to a grinding halt when Reggie, opening the plane's door, gasped, "Great Scott, look there."

Everyone looked and in an instant a big scramble was on. "Oomingmak," garbled one of the Eskimos, meaning the *bearded one*.

We piled out of the plane and made our way toward a greatly startled herd of musk-ox. There was wildlife all around.

"Look there," yelled Paul, "Caribou! Get the caribou. The musk-ox will hold. Get the caribou!"

Bolex in hand and two still cameras dangling from my neck, I turned to photograph the fleeing caribou—six, twelve, twenty animals stampeding away across the barren landscape. They were moving swiftly like mottled gray-white ghosts on a vast barren stage. I turned to film the racing animals when to my utter exasp-

Stampeding Barren Ground caribou.

eration I discovered my view finder blocked. I fumbled and worked
the gadget but couldn't see a thing through it. I said nothing but
inwardly I was tied up in knots. The excitement of seeing all this
wild game and then suddenly finding myself in a predicament made
me desperate. Again and again I tried to adjust the viewer but it
only served to make the tension worse. What's more, with my experience at photography, I felt a little embarrassed. For what
seemed like several critical minutes I wrestled with the view finder
when suddenly the inside control bar became adjusted and I could
see light through it again. But by now the caribou were pretty well
out of filming range. There was nothing else to do now but turn
my attention to the musk-ox.

"Not too close," cautioned Paul, "and don't worry, they'll
hold."

Cameras in hand, Reggie and I moved cautiously toward the
herd of black and white shaggy beasts. The five Eskimos and Paul

and the pilot followed us. The snorting, restless beasts were only about seventy-five yards away and obviously did not like our intrusion and showed it. When our plane landed it had surprised them and they formed quickly into a defense ring. Now ready and waiting they pawed the ground, snorted and fumed. A few large animals were making menacing gestures, heads low, and weaving back and forth. Foot by foot Reggie and I drew closer, now sixty yards, now about fifty. The group began to get defiant and one big bull lunged out more than half his length but quickly backed into his ring again. Paul kept cautioning us to take it easy. My throat felt dry as paper and for long periods of time I hardly seemed to breathe—musk-ox in close view for the first time! Yes, at last, I was face to face with Oomingmak. Soon it was eyeball to eyeball. We still pressed on. Suddenly my mind flashed something to my legs. Would I be ready for a fast sprint if need be? What if several musk-ox charged? Now the distance was in feet— ninety. . .eighty. . .seventy dangerous feet!

The author photographing a musk-ox herd on Bathurst Island in the Canadian Arctic Archipelago.

"Not another foot, you two," screamed Paul, "they'll charge. I know it. They'll charge." With Paul frantic, we held our ground at about sixty-five feet, filming, reloading, snapping all the pictures our cameras would take. Snorting furiously and stamping the ground in formidable gestures, the odorless beasts made a wonderful scene. It was the true Arctic in all its stark wildness.

But the animals did not charge. Instead, in a moment, they bolted away in kind of a confused stampede only to reform once again in about a hundred feet. Reggie and I went after them but kept our distance. It was sheer boundless excitement, all primitive nature every inch of the way. At one point a large bull butted a calf and sent it spinning to the ground, like a stumbled puppy dog. It thrashed there for a moment and was up again bouncing in a second. The incident was comical and it broke the tension for a spell. I was amazed at the speed and agility of these beasts, so quick and utterly fast they were when they needed to be. Little wonder these incredible mammals have learned to survive in this difficult land.

I took a whole series of still pictures and slide shots and then ran out one more roll of film, hoping mentally I had the exposures right. One doesn't find a treat like this very often in the high North Country, and when it does come, using extra film is the least thing to worry about.

Paul explained that our musk-ox group was a small herd and that the island had many like it and larger. As we pressed on toward the beasts once more, just for the fun this time, a gyrfalcon suddenly appeared out of nowhere, fluttered fearlessly around in circles, like a pigeon and landed in front of me, barely twenty feet away. It seemed puzzled. Apparently, the bird had never seen humans before and became curious by all the strange events that were taking place.

Once more we approached the musk-ox and again got so close that they sniffed and snorted and pawed the earth, swaying back and forth. Then I remembered what young Penny said back in Cornwallis and I knew he had been kidding. No, you don't pet these wild beasts. Nor do you even get within living-room distance of them, and anyone who tries it is simply asking for trouble. No, Penny never scratched the head of a live musk-ox.

The gyrfalcon, meanwhile, seemed intrigued by what was going on. Never had I seen a bird act more strangely. In a way I was sorry we had no morsel to offer it, to see how it would react. It

Lone musk-ox on the Arctic tundra.

just stood there, now ten feet away, glaring at my every move. Had I not been so intent on taking more pictures of the musk-ox I would have turned my camera on it. And there is every likelihood that it would have held perfectly still for a long time, enabling me to get some interesting closeups. But I was out of film by now.

I was sure this was the Arctic-ranging gyrfalcon, a member of the hawk tribe said to be very fierce and predacious. These birds are supposed to be so swift as to catch a duck on the wing or be able to overtake a flitting snow bunting. They are known to be powerful enough to crush the spine of a large Arctic hare.

The musk-ox were snorting loudly now and drew my attention away from the bird. I reloaded my still camera and took more shots of the musk-ox, then returned to the gyrfalcon. Reaching out my outstretched hand, I cautiously inched my way to within three feet of the bird when it suddenly pumped its legs and sprung into the air but still apparently unafraid. It flew over the musk-ox and then winged away across the rolling open tundra.

Once more I went to work on the musk-ox. As I approached them this time, they bolted again, raced a good distance, and re-formed for the fourth and last time. It was an old familiar game by now and so we left them alone after that. We had had our day with Oomingmak.

Land of the midnight sun in the central Arctic.

There was work ahead. The Eskimos promptly started to pitch their tents and Paul began unpacking. The sun was sinking low toward the horizon and I could see that Dick was anxious to get away. It was regrettable. Never had I wanted to stay on an Arctic island so much. We bade farewell to Paul and the Eskimos, climbed aboard the Otter, and started off. I sat up front this time with Dick; Reggie sat in back of us. In a few minutes we were up in the air once more over Bathurst Island, winging over the musk-ox which only a few moments before we had annoyed and tested.

The light was still good and Dick began cruising about for a while, pointing out one form of wildlife after another: Peary caribou, musk-ox singles, twos, threes, and some large groups. At one point he dropped low and we looked over the ruins of an old Eskimo settlement, its rocky foundation walls still quite discernable. At another spot Reggie noticed something white scurrying along the ground. "Look, down there," he said. It was a large Arctic hare. It was bounding along in a peculiar fashion. It stood out amazingly white and clear against the gray-bottom tundra and was sort of sprinting like a kangaroo.

Dick glanced down onto his map and then started to make a great turn. He had been checking out his bearing. It was clear that he was heading south back for Resolute. At this point Dick announced we were over the central Arctic Archipelago—"only a bare 840 miles from the North Pole"—our furthest northward penetration.

I sighed. It was truly my finest day in the land beyond the North Wind.

14
Year of the Tuk-tu

The Arctic year begins and ends in darkness. When the spring sun crosses its direct line to the equator and starts its swing across the northern hemisphere, the land of the *tuk-tu* caribou is gripped by the elements, by snow and ice and relentless cold. The nights are much too long to trigger serious changes in the metabolic processes of plants and animals. For the northernmost of the caribou on the tundra life is difficult and monotonous. Those hardy bands who have stayed all winter on the tundra islands have now sought the protection of the lowlands, there to paw through the snow for stunted willows and dwarf birch. These northern species, the Peary caribou, along with small herds of musk-ox, are the only ungulates to brave the Arctic year this far north. Somehow by some miracle small groups of bulls and cows and young of both species have survived. But early spring air says that the nights will shorten and that the longspurs will return. So shall the willows. The tundra will surely turn green again.

As the new year advances the north country becomes shrouded in a kind of semitwilight. The daylight hours remain brief, mostly before and immediately following noon hour. On cloudy days even the short daylight hours seem but a gray glow, like the strangeness of light from the eclipse of the sun. There is deathly silence in this land. The spell is broken only occasionally by the wail of the Arctic wolf or the distant rumble of shifting ice along the frozen sea.

Down in the sub-Arctic taiga the Barren Ground caribou stir about in the spruce forests. The winter fat on the haunches of the once virile males is gone now. Even the oil fat is gone from the bone marrow of the cows. The snow is still deep in the timber, is firm and hard underfoot, and pawing for *Cladonia* moss has gone on for too long.

But the winds of March have come and April days are longer now. There is more light and warmth and a new and restless mood comes to the Arctic. The snowy owl flutters more often, the ptarmigan and Arctic hare seem more restive. More and more lemmings now steal out of their ice-packed burrows and venture onto the wet snow.

The taiga is suddenly astir. The spark of life has been triggered by certain forms of ultraviolet light rays and its effects show. Not

Barren Ground caribou on the Arctic Barrens, Canada.

all plants and animals respond at the same time, nor in the same quiet way. In some forms, like the spruce grouse, the change in more active feeding habits is noticeable. The grouse flies further and stronger and climbs higher in the tops of the aspen to feed on swelling buds. The red squirrel chatters more frequently in the spruce thickets and races more nervously from tree to tree. More lemmings poke their noses out of the breathing holes in the snow and some individuals scurry boldly over the snow's crust. Wings of food-seeking raptors cast their moving shadows over the taiga and the hares in the willow thickets grow nervous.

As the nights shorten still more there is much snorting and crashing in the spruce forests. The caribou are gathering. In bigger and bigger numbers they come, moving through the muskegs, breaking through the snow, grunting, and breaking down branches from the aspen. One morning, days later, the tuk-tu have seemingly left for the open barrens and the scene in the taiga is like a beaten down forest pasture. Urine stains on the snow are everywhere, and dark, almost black pellets pepper all the trails. Shoots of willow and aspen have been chewed off above the snow and thousands of paw holes pockmark the feeding grounds.

The gathering of the caribou along the edge of the dwindling taiga continues on until one moonlit night, in May, a large bull caribou senses a certain something in the air and strikes out boldly across the tundra. Confusion reigns. Some less audacious bands return to the taiga. Others turn around. But the seeming bedlam is brief. The big bull has set the stage and in a few days the northward push is on for certain.

The caribou pour out of the taiga. Out and onto the treeless plains they go, out across the tundra snow, outward and onward. Here and there patches of brown earth appear around the eskers and the caribou flock to it. They commence to feed on the exposed sedges and lichens. More and still more come, sloshing through the now wet snow, forming wide bands of white and mottled brown animal life. Like flowing rocks of the tundra they go, ever moving across the vast emptiness of the windswept plain.

Suddenly, along the flanks of one of the leading bands, several dark forms appear. They are Arctic wolves and they are crowding the caribou. They press inward. The caribou herd tightens and for a while begins to flow more swiftly. But the flow slackens and becomes normal again.

One pregnant cow with a bad hoof lags behind. An old bull, still bleeding from two raw places in his skull where antlers had shed late plus a gash in his side, has a slow gait. The wolf pack presses closer but the consumptive instinct has not yet been fully triggered. All day long the wolves follow the caribou. Then at one point, just before the evening sunset, the largest of the wolves, totally male and easily 180 pounds of muscle and sinew, suddenly sees a ridge of rock and gravel. He pulls ahead of his canine pack and begins a skirting maneuver. He knows the old caribou trail and will travel it. Night comes.

The dawn finds the wolves and caribou still together but now the wolf pack leads the caribou migration. Out front by a good three hundred yards, the canine sixsome moves slowly. The big male looks back over his shoulder now and then and continues a correct pace. The caribou seem unafraid. A small patch of moving fur up front is a common sight and is only to be feared when it turns wild.

Two hours before nightfall the wolf pack again takes a position alongside the moving caribou, now only a safe distance of a hundred yards. The caribou fog is strong and the big male wolf in the lead begins to drop his head. His ears flatten back as he senses the bleeding bull and the limping cow. The hunger mechanism strikes his brain and the attack is on: a lightninglike dash over the tundra, a mighty leap, jaws closing, fur flying and a caribou is down. Other wolves and caribou tangle, hide and fur and blood are mixed up. A double kill is made. The great herd thunders into a mighty stampede, but it lasts only five minutes. A pair of its weaker kind has been culled. The balance of nature has worked again in the Arctic.

One month after the attack, including a lesser encounter with a Barren Ground grizzly, the caribou have come five hundred miles across the tundra. Now the bulls begin to separate from the cows and yearlings. The large females with protruding bellies take to the lowlands, their direction northeasterly. In the flatlands the brown tundra begins to turn green. Snow continues on the lakes and across the north slopes of ridges. As the two great caribou bands split and push onward, warm, sunlit days come. Mosquitoes appear. So do hardy birds from southern climes. Out of the cold mackerel-studded clouds small flocks of white-bodied geese with black wing tips come into view. They're greater snow geese from way down under. They've come two thousand miles from Del-Mar-Va and the Carolinas and they're looking for nesting sites. The open sounds and lakes look promising.

Polar bear is king of the Northland carnivores.

Meanwhile, on one of the northernmost islands, where the smaller groups of Peary caribou and musk-ox have braved eight months of winter, a great white form steals around the pack ice. He is the lord of the carnivores, king of the Polar North, the polar bear. His female counterparts are nowhere to be seen. Their pregnant heaviness has moved them inland toward dry ground to give birth to cubs. At each seal kill the white furred ghost of the Arctic leaves a trail of blood over ice and snow. Many birds—gulls, dovekies, terns, and gyrfalcons—follow it. Across the ice fields and drift ice comes a distant thundering roar as an iceberg calves away and drops a large mass of ice into the melting, frigid sea. The great male polar bear sees several caribou on land, stops, yawns, and lets out a deep-throated bellow. But he is full of seal and is not interested.

Beyond where the caribou graze the white geese are forming. The place is soggy ground near the shelf ice. Now several hundred strong, the flock covers acres, making a strange mixture of lifeless brown tundra and flashing white birdom. Some of the birds begin pairing, others simply wander about listlessly, as if trying to catch a second breath. Those who seem most tired are the latest arrivals. They are silent. When new stragglers arrive out of the cold mists and land, they do not call out their characteristic greeting. Only the strongest geese, the hardiest ganders who had been on northern Baffin for several days, are prone to call out their *ga ga ga ga ga*.

The snow geese strut proudly. They've come a long way to the land beyond the North Wind. Here they will gather until the never-setting sun will take the edge from the permafrost, take it off and send it below the soil crust, and start the saxifrage to bloom and the marsh grasses to green. The pickings for the geese are meager and every bird must forage alone over a wide area for a mouthful of grassy rootstocks and moss. But there is the eternal promise: warmer days will come and the Barrens once more will be fit for geese.

The great journey north is never easy. For ninety-nine and ten days the Back Bay flock, numbering at the start some one thousand birds, kept pretty well together, over the northeastern states, New England, and the Canadian Maritimes. Even at St. Joachim, on the St. Lawrence, where spring grasses are abundant, the flock remained together. But the journey from southern Quebec north was telling. One by one the strongest ganders led a group away never again to be seen except perhaps on the northwestern coast of Greenland, and on Devon and Ellesmere in the Canadian Archipelago.

The flock on Baffin numbered only a fraction of the ten thousand snows that wintered in Virginia. Nature ordained it that way. Northern breeding grounds had to be scattered because natural food was scarce and good nesting places few and far between.

As the nights give up their darkness and sunlit days take over, the snows grow restless. By early June the birds are paired off and the serious business of mating and egg laying is on in full swing. Most of the geese seek out the ponds and lakelets away from the main ice, laying first one, then two, finally a total of six or seven eggs. The eggs are grouped together in a tight circle, partially concealed with dead grass, moss, and feathers.

June comes and the sun rides high. Now it never even sets. Down on the mainland tundra where the big caribou herds have split, the cows reach the calving grounds. The land is a lush pasture of the green, presummer Arctic. Each cow singles out a small plot of sedge-draped ground, twitches and strains and drops a newborn wet calf. The infant animal is almost helpless, a small version of its mother. Now and then a cow drops two. In a few hours the young, wobbly but spirited, are sucking milk. In two days the

Migrating Barren Ground caribou on the Arctic tundra.

calves are strong enough to follow their mothers. The scent from the calving caribou is faint and the wolves do not seem to be around.

But the calving grounds attract abundant wildlife. Some newborn caribou succumb to the cold nights; others are stillborn—and their carcasses are food for a variety of flesh eaters, for the Arctic fox, snowy owl, long-tailed jaeger, wolverine, ermine, and even the lemming. The lemming is not after the meat but after caribou pellets which contain partially digested seeds of sedge. Moreover the green sedge itself, its juicy stalks and rootlets, are now more abundant.

Back down on the mainland tundra, a hundred miles south of the calving grounds, another drama of nature is under way. A lone wolverine has spotted a mother musk-ox and a calf and makes a quick attack. But the shaggy-maned beast drives the wolverine off with her hooves and then herds her young toward a rocky ridge.

The evening sunset over the Arctic tundra.

The big weasellike attacker follows. But the cow ox and her off-spring race for a ridge where seven other musk-ox join them. The group quickly forms into a formidable defense ring, horns and heads presenting a barrier that seem too much for the wolverine. He senses defeat and scurries off.

As the summer days peak the Arctic has become alive with wildlife—whales and porpoises surface here and there between the ice floes, flocks of shorebirds and waterfowl wing from one feeding ground to another. More lemmings appear and after them are white foxes, ermine, owls, falcons, and jaegers.

By late August frosty nights come to the tundra. The geese have brought off their young and have molted. Their new flight feathers are well on their way. The caribou bands have reunited. Some bulls sniff the northwind, turn around for the last time, and begin moving south. Their pace is rapid now. The shorebirds and song-birds have felt the sting of Arctic sleet and are gone. In two weeks the geese fly. Last to leave are the seabirds, the gulls and murres and dovekies. They are short-distance travelers and so their journey to warmer climes is not hurried.

Throughout September and October the caribou have gathered and moved ever southward, eventually to reach the protection of the taiga, there to feed on the boughs of fir and spruce and willow, and to paw through the snow once more after reindeer moss. Out on the Barrens the late autumn days are short. Once it snows and freezes, there is no more thawing, no more letting up of the relentless cold. It just keeps coming on until night and day and cold all seem one. Once again the elements take over: the long frigid nights, the biting wind, ice, and snow. Now the whole land takes on a desolate appearance. For a short time the caribou pour out of the taiga and take to running about. They are rutting. The males with swollen necks are seeking out the females and mounting them. For several weeks the mating goes on until the males are spent and both bulls and cows feel the sting of the North Wind. It is time to return to the protection of the taiga. The big stir of life on the tundra has come to an end. Now only small groups of musk-ox are seen on the open tundra, and here and there an occasional white wolf on some lofty esker, sniffing the polar wind anxiously. The smaller animals, the white fox, Arctic hare, snowy owl remain active. So do the lemmings in their burrows under the snow.

As the full blast of the winter spreads over the tundra world the female white goliath seeks the protection of some ice cave, first to have a partial sleep, then to give birth to her very small polar bear cubs. No more do the Barrens show any caribou, for all who are alive are in the taiga. Now the long nights have come. Now the unhurried dark phase of an unrelenting cycle has arrived. It is part of the Arctic almanac of the Far North—a year of seasonal folding and unfolding, a saga without beginning or real end, the spin of a timeless world where all is nature and everything is bent to it.